In the same series

surfing, grégory maubé - sylvain cazenave
skateboarding, fabrice le mao – mathias fennetaux

© Fitway Publishing, 2005
Original editions in French, English, Spanish, Italian

All rights reserved, including partial or complete translation,
adaptation and reproduction rights, in any form and for any purpose.

Translation by Translate-A-Book, Oxford

Design and creation: GRAPH'M/Nord Compo, France

ISBN: 2-7528-0139-4
Publisher code: T00139

Copyright registration: April 2005

Printed in Singapore by Tien Wah Press

www.fitwaypublishing.com

Fitway Publishing – 12, avenue d'Italie – 75627 Paris cedex 13, France

extreme Sports

kitesurfing

marc bory

Table of Contents

Preface 6

The Thrill of the New 8
The Origins of Kitesurfing 8
A Whole New Experience 12
Manu Bertin: Tribute to a Founding Father 16
Constant Evolution 24

The Kitesurfing Ethos 26
Pioneer Spirit 26
Coming of Age 37
Party-Time 42
Choosing the Right Equipment 44

Kitesurfing Modes 48
The Quest for Self-Expression 48
Freeriding and Tripping 51
Surf and Wave 55
Wakeboard 60
Speed Crossing 63
Speed Racing 64
Freestyle 66
Snowkiting 70

Kitesurfing Icons 72
Robby Naish: Legend and King 74
Teiva Joyeux: Happy-Go-Lucky 78
Charles Deleau: Going For It 82

Martin Vari: Man of Mystery	86	**The Ultimate**	111
Raphaël Salles: Pushing the Envelope	88	'Jaws' (Maui, Hawaii)	111
Fabienne d'Ortoli: A Seasoned Pro	92		
Charlotte Consorti: A Lifestyle Choice	96	**Learning the Craft**	112
Daphnée Laliberté: Following Her Star	102		
		Do It Right or Not at All!	114
The Legendary Top Spots	106		
Maui, Hawaii	106	**Appendices**	116
Cabarete, Dominican Republic	108	Kite-Speak	116
Leucate-La Franqui, France	108	Further Reading	119
Ponte Preta, Cape Verde Islands	109	Acknowledgements	120
Tarifa, Spain	109	Photographic credits	120
North and South Brazil	110		
The Cape, South Africa	110		

Preface

'Kitesurfing', 'kiteboarding', 'flysurfing' – call it what you will depending on the country you're in or the language you speak – these and similar labels all denote an emerging sport that often hits the headlines. Written off in the 1990s by the media and the surfing public at large, kitesurfing has taken off with a vengeance with the dawn of the new Millennium.

One might ask what makes kitesurfing so appealing. The answer, in a word, is that it is *different*. It is new, original, fascinating and quintessentially extreme. And it triggers a sustained and undiluted surge of sheer adrenaline like no other extreme sport.

This book is dedicated to those kitesurfing aficionados who get their kicks either from the sheer acrobatic techniques involved or, quite simply, from the beautiful locations where the sport is practised. But the book and its illustrations are also dedicated to those who love surfing in general and who may wish to discover for themselves the intrinsic elegance of this new variant. If you're in this latter category, then take the plunge *now* and start learning about a sport that is novel yet constantly evolving in terms of technique and equipment.

The following pages are written as a tribute to all those out there who pioneered kitesurfing as a whole new experience, savouring a heady cocktail mixed from equal portions of surfing, kiting, windsurfing and wakeboarding. It doesn't get any better than that!

It is hoped that the illustrations in this volume will give the reader some sense of the astonishingly beautiful locations throughout the world where kitesurfers ply their craft. This isn't a how-to-do-it manual dedicated to teaching the tricks of the kitesurfing trade; instead, it is a celebration of a world of colour, a world of the extreme …

The Origins of Kitesurfing

The sport of kitesurfing can be traced back not to one point of origin but to several. That said, it was essentially developed by a group of water-sports fanatics who were searching for a new way to surf and fly. This is not to imply they were all motivated to the same degree or even that they all pulled in the same direction. The Breton brothers Bruno and Dominique Legaignoux from Quimper in the Finistère region of Northwest France may lay claim to the distinction of being the first to explore the radically new concept of a traction 'wing' capable of touching down and taking off again. After various experiments, the Legaignoux brothers patented their initial *voile marine* ('flysurf') first in France (1984) and then internationally (1985). The new technology featured an inflatable canvas sail stretched across a frame. A prime initial consideration was safety and, for Bruno Legaignoux in particular, the inflatable traction kite system was originally conceived as a means of towing a vessel whose engine had given out or which had shed its sails. The idea was that a skipper could run out the kite and continue to make headway, albeit uncertainly, riding out a storm, for example, until help arrived. This explains why the first two-line kite wing was christened Wipi Cat (from WInd-Powered Inflatable CATamaran), a forerunner of the now universally known commercial brand Wipika (WInd-Powered Inflatable Kite Aircraft).

Bruno and Dominique Legaignoux envisaged a whole series of other and, generally speaking, more playful watercraft applications for their invention, but their wing fell short in terms of accurate steering and upwind navigation. It was not until the late 1990s that a French windsurfing professional called Manu Bertin hit on the notion of hitching a kite to a surfboard. He later claimed he got the idea from the surreal sight of a catamaran being towed by a series of kites during the *Semaine de Vitesse* speed regatta in Brest in 1982.

Bruno and Dominique Legaignoux, 1984.

The Thrill of the New

Bertin had already experimented with steering by kite and by means of flexible 'caisson' wings and, when he heard about the Legaignoux brothers and their *voile marine*, he immediately asked them if he could try it out. At the time, only a small number of wings had been produced at the brothers' workshop in Brittany, but they readily agreed to lend Bertin one or two for trial purposes. The early 1990s found Bertin in Hawaii in the august company of legendary Hawaiian surfer Laird Hamilton. They were poised to test the inflatable wing harnessed to a surfboard for the very first time. It is Bertin who must be credited with refining the Legaignoux technology to enable the kitesurfer to launch from a specific point and return to it. Similarly, it was input from Bertin that resulted in four-line steering and a control bar specially designed for it, and progressively sophisticated and streamlined boards.

A first attempt by a sailing and windsurfing firm to commercialise the new technology was abandoned because research was progressing too slowly. Then Robby Naish, who had dominated the windsurfing industry for the better part of 15 years, finally decided to invest in kitesurfing, inspired no doubt by the sight of Manu Bertin slicing through the waves off Maui's North Shore. Naish signed a licensing agreement with the Legaignoux brothers in 1996 and committed himself to commercialising the technology under the Naish brand, alongside his windsurfing product range. His success has since prompted numerous competitors to throw their hats into the ring, among them Raphaël Salles, another ex-professional windsurfer, who is credited with launching the first-ever 100% kitesurfing company, F-One. Salles has emerged as a technical innovator *par excellence* and, both as a kitesurfer in his own right and as a technical adviser to the sport, has developed a range of floats and wings ('kites' in surfer parlance) that are now being marketed with conspicuous success.

Laird Hamilton, 1996.

A Whole New Experience

Kitesurfing has proved an inspiration to a whole generation of high-level performers who have embraced the sport as practitioners and innovators. Nothing is too far out, it seems. Take Bruno Sroka and Fabienne d'Ortoli, for example, who – together with their 'shaper', Thierry Le Corre – spent untold hours in 2002 and 2003 studying and developing tandem kitesurfing. This was a whole new experience – sharing the same surf-glide *and* sharing the risks of tangled lines, mid-air collisions and reduced control in exchange for increased traction. A small price to pay, of course, for the indescribable exhilaration of kitesurfing *à deux*.

To get this project – literally – off the ground, Bruno and Fabienne had to come up with a modified board that enabled two kitesurfers to stand sufficiently close to each other in order to 'bond' yet sufficiently far apart so as to be able to manoeuvre independently. They tested the system time and again over and in the translucent waters of the Aber-Wrach estuary in northwest Brittany, wrestling with the basic problem of how to synchronise a two-kite water start. Like the development of its windsurfing cousin back in the 1980s, tandem kitesurfing takes as its point of departure an idea that is as simple in theory as it is bold in practice. It is a novel and spectacular experience watching two kitesurfers interfacing on a single board or on tandem boards.

Right-hand page: *Tandem kitesurfing calls for coordinated skills and mutual understanding.*

Coordination and anticipation: Leading from the front.

Manu Bertin:
Tribute to a Founding Father

Ex-windsurfing pro Manu Bertin is the undisputed pioneer of kitesurfing and, to the extent that he is unquestionably the sport's founding father, it is interesting to learn why and how he made the transition. In all probability, it all comes down to his taste for adventure and his enthusiasm for change. For Bertin, windsurfing had run its course by the early 1990s. Funding for the professional circuit was starting to dry up in the wake of a media ban on alcohol and tobacco advertising during sporting broadcasts. Worse, perhaps, was the prospect of continuing to trek around the world, often at one's own expense, lugging all the voluminous and heavy gear and ancillary equipment that windsurfing entails. Besides, there was the added hassle of negotiating excess baggage charges with airlines that appeared to rewrite the ground rules as and when they saw fit. For the likes of Manu Bertin, the time had come to rethink, reassess priorities, perhaps even change tack. In the late 1980s, he had already toyed with the idea of surfing on a kite-powered board. To start the ball rolling, he drew on his connections in the windsurfing world and on his own considerable experience as technical director of a leading Australian sail manufacturer.

In full flow: 'Carving' enables taking off again at top speed.

In hostile territory: Team No Limits member Manu Bertin on the set in Hawaii for a 'Sector' brand promotional film.

THE THRILL OF THE NEW

And of course he had the advantage of his own surfing skills acquired over the years. Bertin then cast about for financial backers to underwrite this new extreme sport and, before long, he was performing alongside free-fall parachutist Patrick Gaillardon in Italy's famous Team No Limits. Under its auspices, Bertin embarked on a series of challenges, including surfing among the icebergs off Greenland and traversing in a howling gale from Big Island to Maui in the Hawaiian archipelago. As this volume went to press, another challenge loomed, a challenge destined to put body, heart and soul to the ultimate test: crossing the Atlantic solo, no less. Manu Bertin has already embarked on a strenuous training schedule involving 'short hops' across the Mediterranean from Cap Camarat in the Var to Calvi in the north of Corsica.

The Atlantic Project has 'Manu Bertin' written all over it. It is typical of the man to continually seek out fresh challenges and take on what has never before been attempted. The Atlantic Ride is only one in a long list of projects Bertin has pencilled in to test not only equipment and logistics but also the limits of human endurance. His passion for riding giant waves in the open ocean is second nature to him – as it is for so many of today's pioneering kitesurfers.

Opposite: *An exceptional moment: Cruising as the Sun dips towards the horizon …*

Double-page spread overleaf: *Manu Bertin at Ho'ikipa, Maui, Hawaii (December 2002).*

Constant **Evolution**

Ever since kitesurfing caught on and fired the imagination, its prime movers and exponents have invested heavily in developing add-ons and improving surfing techniques, the aim being to help kitesurfers everywhere make optimal use of their equipment and, by extension, their talents. Today, the sport has its professionals and a host of technical advisers who are all driven by one overriding ambition, namely to boost performance at the competitive end. Some ingenious innovations – such as the twin tip board, which replaced the surf-type board, fixed board leash systems adapted for use with wakeboards, or waist-high safety harness attachments to permit greater flexibility when executing aerial acrobatics – have already found their way into commercial mass production.

In addition to the pros, however, there are still legions of dedicated part-time kitesurfers who get slowly better weekend by weekend as they assimilate the ins and outs of the sport, such as how to trim the kite in full flight or how to manipulate the power/depower shackle to boost speed. Others focus on specific safety aspects, such as the quick-release feature introduced by the simple expedient of adding a Wichard snap-hook. Others still envisage technical improvements to afford a measure of greater kitesurfer autonomy, such as a fifth line, which, this year, is a fixture on every brand that has not developed its own customised form of safety system. Overall, the big drive at the mass market level is towards enhanced safety features. Kitesurfing is a high-risk pastime, after all, but one in which risks can be significantly mitigated by the staged introduction of safety features. A prime requirement in this respect is that kite and board leashes can be disengaged as and when necessary. There are all manner of other innovations in the pipeline as ongoing research seeks ways to make the sport safer and more accessible. Particular mention should be made in this respect of the comprehensive codes of conduct which govern kitesurfing and its devotees, together with coaching programmes available

Hang-time: What could be more spectacular?

Taking a breather at Kitebeach Park, Maui.

from instructors qualified at national federation level or under the auspices of international organisations currently being set up. This all bodes well for the future in terms of teaching both kitesurfing basics and proper respect for the locations and communities where this extreme sport is increasingly practised and enjoyed.

Pioneer Spirit

It is often alleged that kitesurfers have something unusual about their genetic make-up, and that would certainly account for the passionate commitment to the sport exhibited by professionals and part-timers alike. Whatever the reason, however, they did not take to kitesurfing on a whim. Almost invariably, the top-flight kitesurfers are sportsmen and sportswomen of long standing who have taken a conscious decision to try out this new genre. The plain fact is that even top athletes are constantly nagged by doubt as to their chosen discipline and that, irrespective of their age, they agonise over ways and means to enhance their performance. Reaching the top in any profession frequently presupposes hours of training and may entail substantial financial hardship and a circumscribed social life. What, they often ask themselves, is to prevent them going stale? And what can be done to free themselves from the inherent or self-imposed constraints in their chosen careers? Kitesurfing may well prove the answer to these and related questions. There is no great mystery involved – all it takes is a couple of kites, a board, a harness and a control bar. Granted, professional kitesurfers may have to put up with a degree of inconvenience as they travel with all their gear from one hotspot to another and struggle to adapt to local conditions, but this is their cho ce in order to indulge in an alternative to other types of sport. What is more, kitesurfing competence can be achieved comparatively quickly. It is addictive, that much is certain, and those drawn to this sporting Eldorado (and talented and brave enough to explore it) are amply rewarded. Not least, kitesurfing creates a unique sense of belonging to an informal community of equals who bond to share enthusiasms and pleasures. Kitesurfers have formed a community of individualists that has spawned its own code of conduct, its own jargon, its own sense of values and tastes, and its own brand of mutual respect.

Franz Olry bottoming out. His equipment is uncomplicated and does not impair his vision.

The Kitesurfing Ethos

The sheer pleasure of kitesurfing is virtually an end in itself, however. It represents a release of pent-up aspirations and energy. Some channel this energy into competition, an aspect of the sport that has done much to ensure its growing popularity, but, even there, pleasure derives as much from entertaining one's fellow kitesurfers as it does from impressing a jury.

Kitesurfing is a thrilling pursuit. At its highest level, it is an intoxicating three-dimensional mix of aerial and water sports, whose choreography appears to defy both gravity and space as the kite loops and swoops and the rider gyrates around the bar. Here, the launch, ride and touchdown sequence has become second nature, incidental almost. But there are other less extreme forms of kitesurfing, where the principal element is water and where the rider, in a constant quest for acceleration, surfs the waves freestyle. No matter what the level of expertise, a feeling of elation and freedom is triggered by the surge of adrenaline brought on by fresh emotions and fresh experiences.

Kitesurfing is practised in a wide variety of surroundings – on the flat, in the mountains, on hillsides and on sand dunes. Wherever it takes place, newcomers bring a personal style and skills that give a new dimension to the sport.

Above *Determination personified: Suzie Mai executes a high tail-grab.*

Left-hand page: *Traction peaks at 360° downwnd; on the right, Rémi Branco performs a big one-hand Railey.*

THE KITESURFING ETHOS

Windsurfing is the sport that has given kitesurfing most of its devotees and champions. A person's windsurfing background is evident from some of his or her mid-air moves and at times a tentative and experimental approach to kite-drawn wave surfing. Many ex-windsurfers – Robby Naish, Charles Deleau or Hervé Bouré among them – still windsurf but tend to do so only on rare occasions and when the weather conditions are absolutely right.

At the end of the 1990s, when they took up kitesurfing, they made rapid headway because the two disciplines were clearly related. Not only did they assimilate kitesurfing techniques, but they also imposed their own particular style and approach. It comes as no great surprise that there are remarkable similarities between windsurfing and kitesurfing moves, with the former's table-tops, backloops, frontloops, off-the-lip and other figures now complemented by specific kitesurfing elements such as freestyle and big air.

These windsurfers and others like them have exhibited a phenomenal ability to adapt and make the grade at the highest international level. That they have been able to do so is down to their dedication and perseverance. Like Manu Bertin before them, they worked long and hard to assimilate the specifics of kitesurfing and to bring to the sport that permutation of personality and forward-looking creativity that is the mark of true champions.

Kite-Flying is a vital element of first-rank kitesurfing and some kite-flyer experts are able to draw on long years of intensive practice that are a tremendous advantage when handling a kite, irrespective of prevailing meteorological conditions. When it comes to wave surfing, however, they tend to favour light-to-moderate wind conditions as they seek to match their talents in the air to the demands of the water.

Take Etienne Lhote, a twenty-two-year-old who is already a kitesurfing point of reference. He was number two in France in 2003 and competes in international events coordinated by the PKRA (Professional Kite Riders Association), one of the two current professional circuits. To date, his best results have been a fifth at Fuerteventura in the Canary Islands and a seventh place overall in 2004.

Lhote's style is perhaps best described as 'radical' and his ambition, simply put, is to go higher and further. He is an accomplished kite-flyer with an acute awareness of space and an uncommon precision in terms of choosing the right lines and coping with obstacles – real and imaginary. He is noted particularly for his kite-loops and other figures and appears totally at home in the air, producing moves that are fluent, technically accomplished and frequently breathtaking.

Above: An off-the-lip from Julien: Who has got it right – the windsurfer or the kitesurfer?

Left-hand page: Hervé Bouré at re-entry: Waves are not only for surfers and windsurfers …

Wakeboarding is closely related to kitesurfing and switching from one discipline to the other is more often than not motivated by nothing more than a desire to achieve autonomy, which is to say, to cut oneself free of the speedboat and all its attendant noises and smells. Piloting a large traction kite is a whole new experience for wakeboarders, and it does not mean a negation of their personal style. In practice, wakeboarders tend to be younger than the average kitesurfer, but the benchmark personalities in the highly physical discipline of wakeboarding are incontestably two of its pioneers, Lou Wainman and Shannon Best.

Left-hand page: *Étienne Lhote executes a one-foot tai.-grab.*

Below: *Wake-style pioneer Lou Wainman lives it up at home in Maui.*

Double-page spread overleaf: Top *Mika rules the airways*; Bottom *Wake-style is radical and committed – here, Betrand Fleury performs a low-wing backroll*; Right *Extreme manoeuvre Wakeboard-style – Teiva Joyeux pulls a big Railey.*

THE KITESURFING ETHOS

In kitesurfing circles, Lou Wainman is regarded as a one-off: a creative and innovative water-sports enthusiast whose style is distinctly wakeboard-oriented – even to the point of opting for a two-line board with wakeboard rails. His rotations are tight and controlled, ultra-rapid and highly stylised. He has his admirers and his disciples, although there are kitesurfers who find his style too radical and, as a result, dangerous. Dual-line navigation *à la* wakeboard is an exhausting business (each set lasts fifteen to twenty minutes) but Lou Wainman's gruelling training programme means he can cope with these physical demands. To add some spice to the proceedings, Wainman has recently experimented with snowkiting which, by all accounts, he finds highly rewarding. Shannon Best, another wakeboard stylist, competes at the highest level and currently coaches at a kitesurfing school in North Carolina (USA).

Gymnastics is another sports discipline which has had an impact on kitesurfing as practitioners strive to integrate its grace and elegance. For them, kitesurfing at the highest level does not preclude these qualities but should seek to embrace them. Mika came to the notice of a wider public by incorporating carefully executed gymnastics-inspired moves into his freestyle runs and, at the competitive level, there is every reason to believe that those who insert such moves into their routines may have an edge over many of their rivals. For Mika, at least, kitesurfing is an art form. The time he lavishes on refining and perfecting a particular kitesurfing move would be unthinkable in a windsurfing or wakeboarding context. Mika has upgraded and diversified his repertoire to the point where, as of 2004, he has now been admitted to membership of the exclusive inner circle of kitesurfers who battle it out each autumn at the Red Bull King of the Air final in Hawaii. Mika's attitude and approach are living proof that technical expertise need not preclude elegance and beauty.

Coming of Age

The language of the media has had a substantive role to play in the emergence and propagation of kitesurfing to the extent that this new and extreme sport and its audience have come to be identified in terms of a specific aesthetic. The sport's marketing potential is now recognised not only in its own right but in a much wider context. Today, the image of kitesurfing has been used in advertising such diverse products as cars, confectionery, beverages, clothing, telecoms, hi-fi and so on – in every case, seeking to project a youthful and dynamic 'with-it' image.

Above: *Dropping down a white-foam wall, one of many options on the Landes coast in southwest France.*

Left-hand page: *Richard Boudia in action. Wave-riding is a joy for those who love the sea …*

Opposite: Individualism is a sign of our times: Kitesurfing seeks out new sensations (Audi, 2004) ...

Right-hand page: Verging on the surreal: Franz Olry at the office.

Every sports discipline has its own specific identity and values that, inevitably, accrue and attach to those involved in it. And kitesurfing is no exception. Devotees of the sport project a powerful image as passionate and committed members of a trendy generation – all the more so, it seems, because of kitesurfing's disparate origins. What is more, kitesurfing reaches out to an increasingly media-oriented, not to say media-obsessed, generation. As a result, the sport exerts a fascination not so much for a specific 'movement' as for a whole series of related interest (and, above all, consumer) groups. So much is evident from the proliferation of car stickers, logos, T-shirts and other accessories, which proclaim to all and sundry a particular attitude and lifestyle.

This process of identification and assimilation is nowhere more evident than in clothing. Dress codes are today a mark of belonging, a passport, as it were. In the case of kitesurfers, it may be said that they like to set themselves apart in terms of apparel and, in consequence, tend to be highly distinctive. They are easily recognisable and, in a word, exude a particular and colourful flamboyance that is very much in keeping with their sport and its acrobatic aspects. Two kitesurfers coming together on a beach for the first time will quickly strike up a rapport when they recognise in each other the subtleties of their

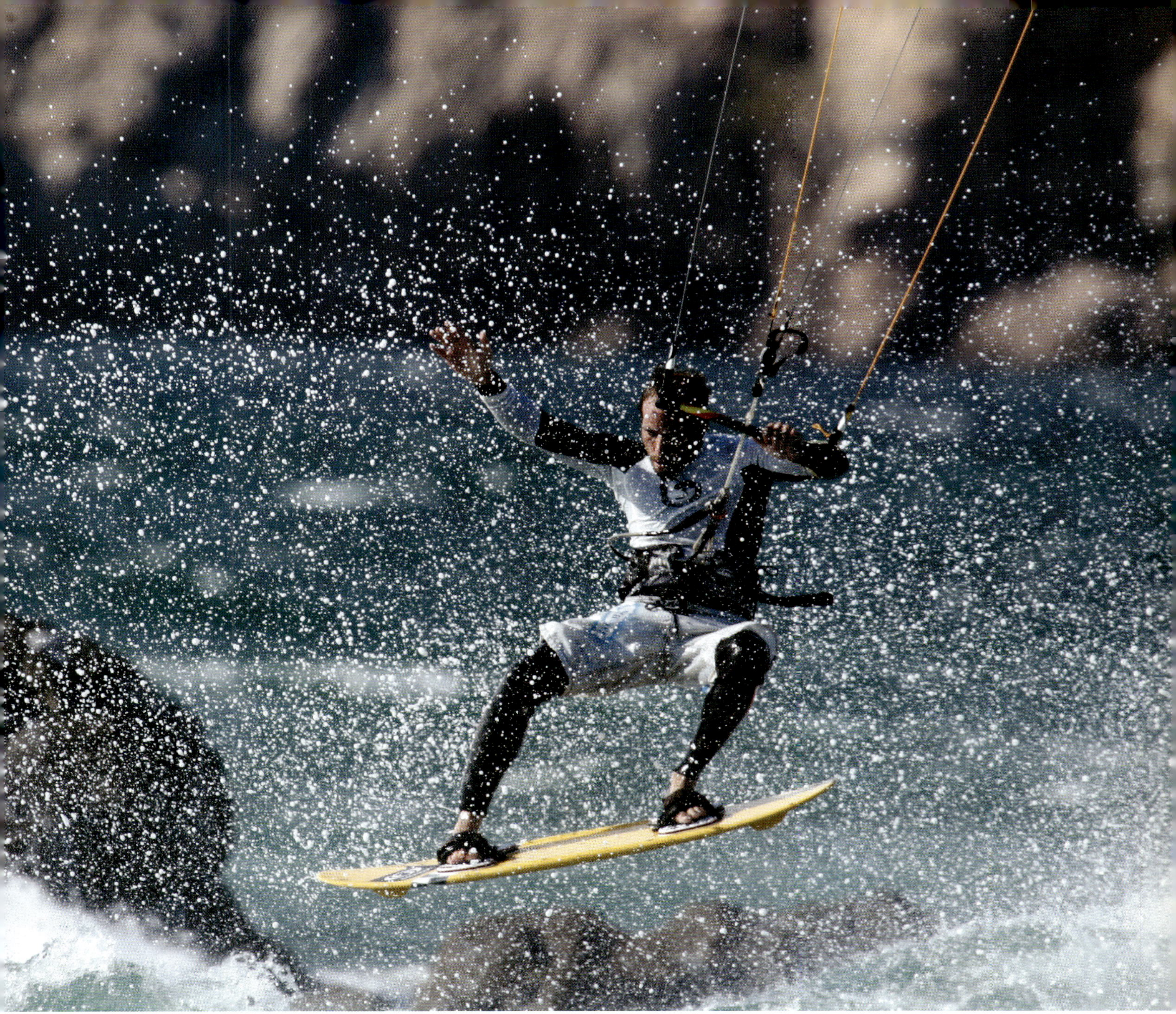

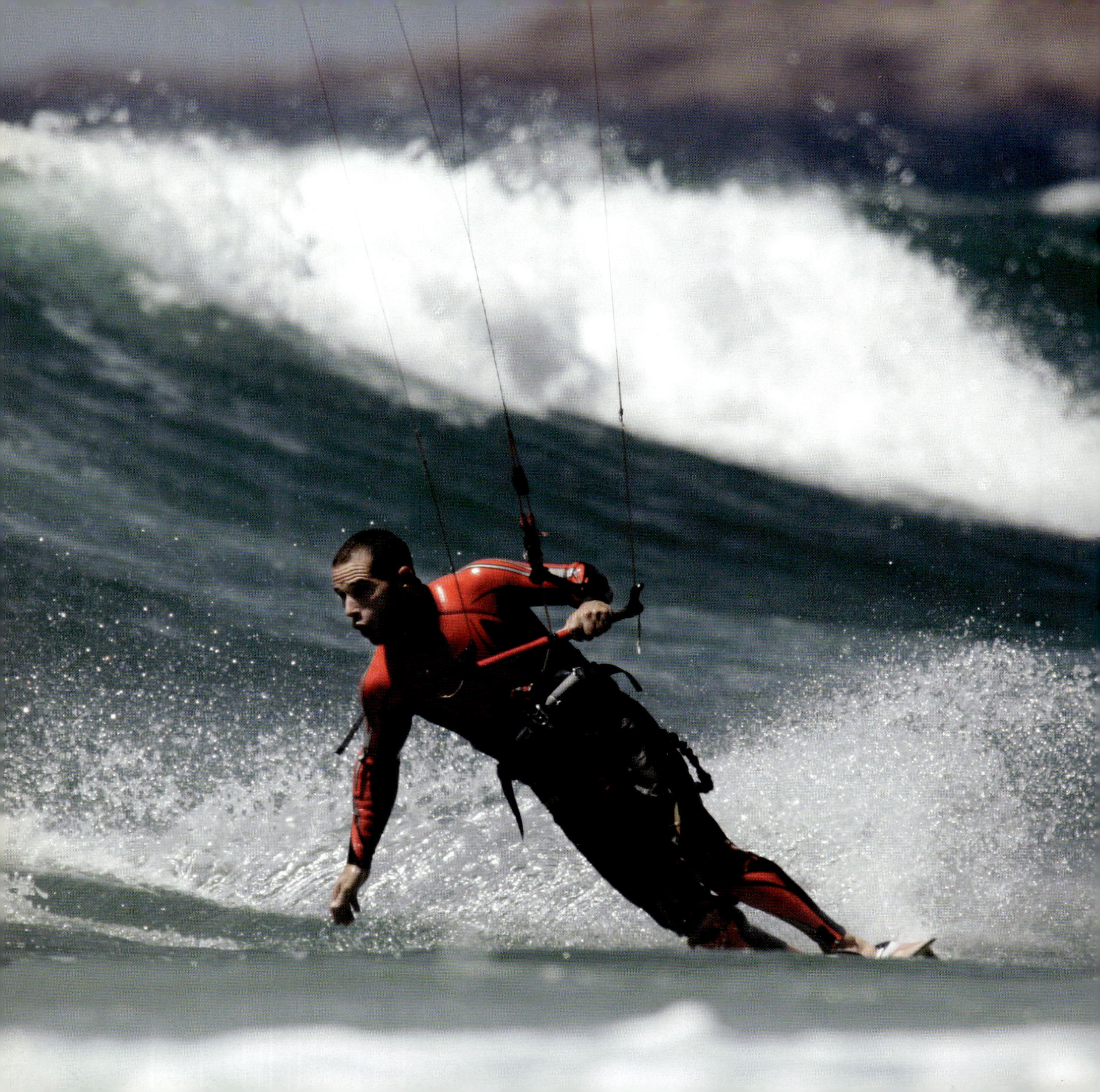

dress code. From then on in, everything changes and a relationship is very quickly cemented.

When the physical exertions of the day are behind them, athletes or sports buffs will typically extend their sense of community and comradeship into the ensuing leisure time, getting together with those of a like mind, sharing experiences and swapping anecdote and gossip. Clearly, their clothing will reflect different sports and cultural backgrounds, but two major trends can be pinpointed worldwide. One is a conscious or instinctive identification with beachwear and surfwear; major clothing manufacturers have been quick to capitalise on this, marketing the image of the sport's ambassadors and the kind of clothes they wear. In the water, the image is basically driven by freestyle or freeride, and it is the same with the 'skateboard look', which tends to be very casual, verging on grunge, in line with the predominantly young skateboarder fraternity's essentially 'laid-back' and 'far-out' attitude to life in general. The other 'look' is more urbane and dictated by current trends in fashion: there are no concessions here to the traditional surfing image, but rather a nod in the direction of urban chic and a more materialistic approach to life. Whatever: kitesurfers from every background seem to be able to congregate and understand one another by a process not unlike that of primitive initiation rites which enable individuals in a tribe to bond swiftly and effectively.

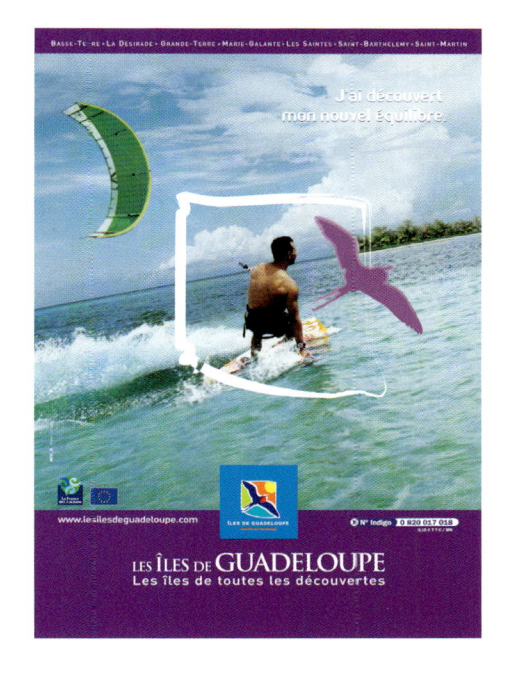

Above: Kitesurfing in marvellous Guadeloupe in Winter 2004: A must for aficionados.

Left-hand page: Concentration: A committed Julien Sudrat gauges the next point of impact.

Party-Time

It doesn't take much: no particular pretext is required, no special occasion. After a day's kitesurfing at some hotspot or other, it seems the most natural thing in the world to get together and shoot the breeze, have a drink or two or even more, grab a bite to eat and stay up for as long as possible, letting the chips fall where they may. Who knows where the evening may end? In a disco, perhaps, where one can dance the night away and even talk – although there is the risk of being drowned out by the music. But, wherever, strangers are welcome and quickly accepted, and perhaps even just as quickly forgotten. Sharing values is where it's all at and this tribe is effectively a closed society that is open to all comers. No one cares how long the festivities last as long as there is 'good wind' tomorrow …

Opposite and right-hand page: *Dance, trance or myth? Kitesurfers letting their hair down at a staging post* en route.

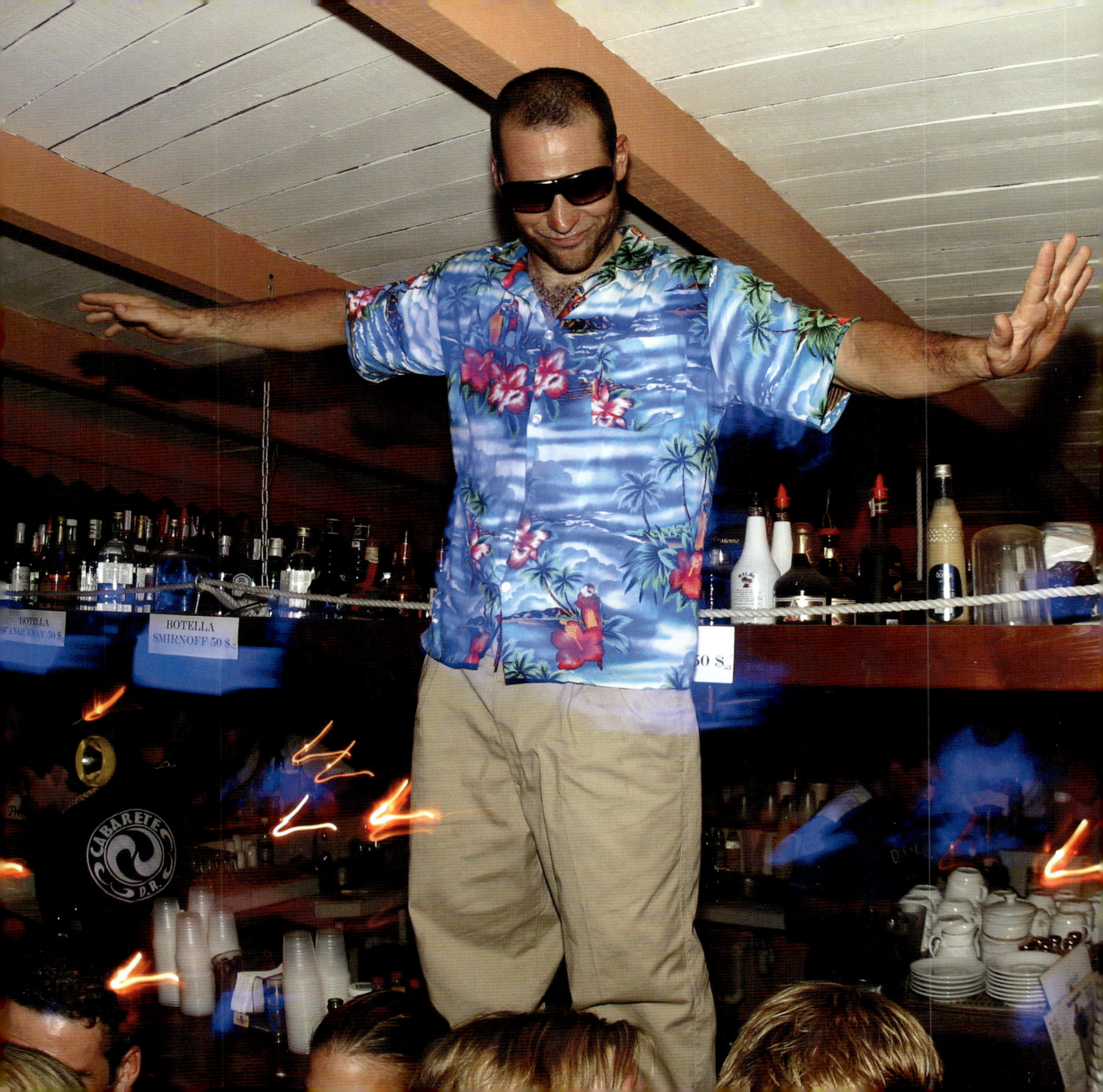
BOTELLA
BOTELLA
SMIRNOFF 50 $
CABARETE
D.R.

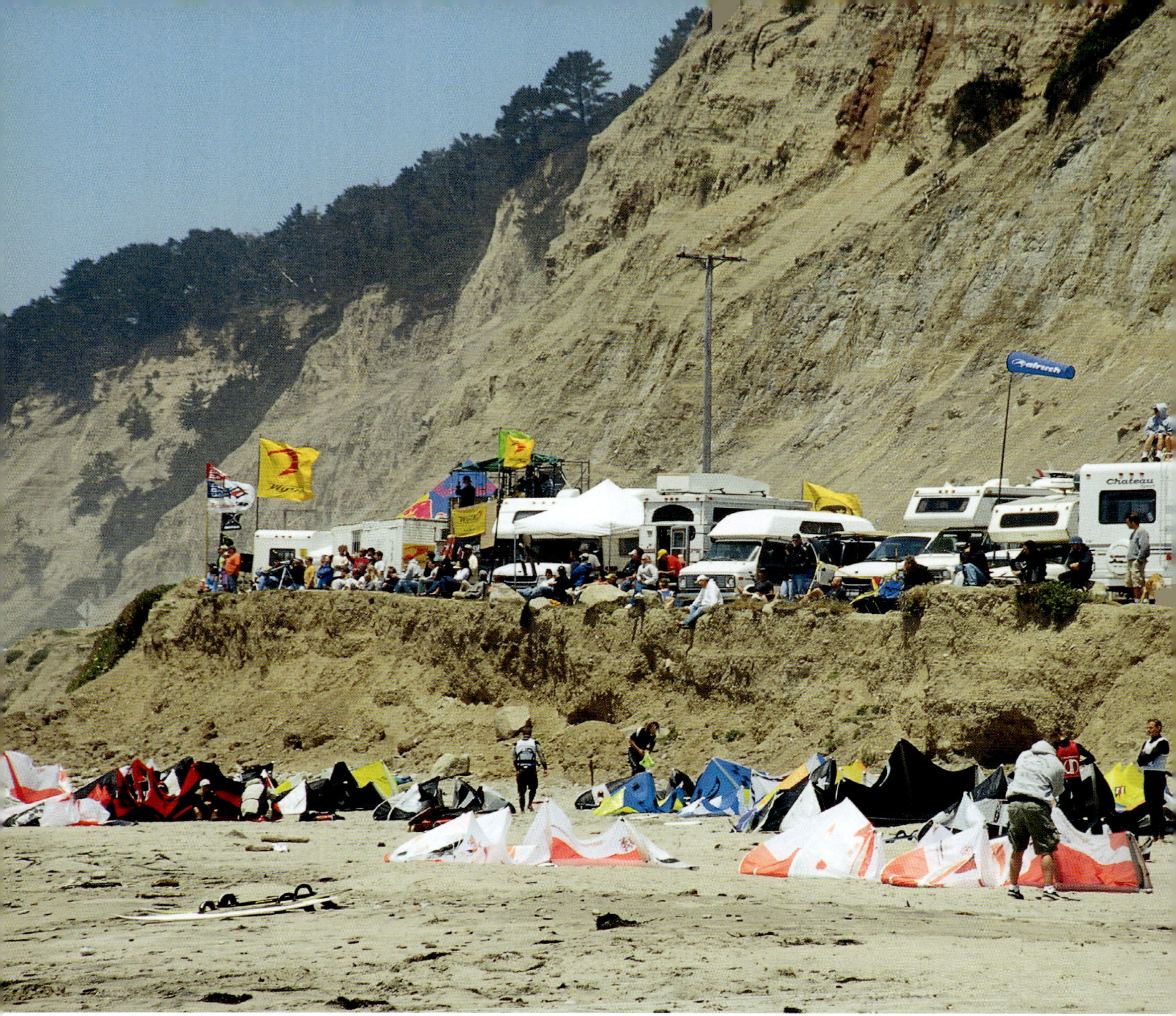

Choosing
the Right Equipment

Novices rack their brains trying to decide what kind of kitesurfing gear to select. Who can blame them? All the reasons they had for getting involved in this new sport seem to crowd in on them when it comes down to selecting equipment to buy. Discovering this new sports discipline and shrugging off all the hassle of surfing and the logistics of wakeboarding may be one thing, but buying one's first set of kitesurfing gear is quite another. On the one hand, there is the understandable desire to purchase solid equipment commensurate with their beginner's status but, on the other, there is that equally understandable inclination to buy gear that makes a *statement*, that pre-empts scathing comments by the initiated. What is it to be? Twin-tip? Middle-of-the-road aspect ratio? Two-line, four-line or five? Whatever the decision, it's ephemeral. There is no such thing as the 'right equipment'. First purchases will not last for ever and there will always be a nagging temptation to upgrade, if for no other purpose than show. Appearances and design specs exert an enormous influence on choice for seasoned veterans and beginners alike. At some hotspots, new faces put in an appearance fresh out of kitesurfing school but already kitted out with the very latest gear imaginable. They are so anxious to assert their new status that they have fallen hook, line and sinker for whatever is trumpeted as being 'new' in the marketplace. They know, of course, that this year's models will be out of fashion next year, but who cares? It doesn't cost all that much to replace what one has.

For the experts, things are very different. They are at least one step ahead when it comes down to analysing their own specific needs, and their choices

Competition time: A plethora of new equipment is unveiled …

(Nearly) everything is possible with the right gear – but keep a weather eye open for grains of sand!

are dictated by a thorough awareness of the technical specifications, grades and material ranges best adapted to their specific requirements. Wisely, they talk to their peers, sharing experiences and test results in terms of boards, kites and control bars. They research the pros and cons of safety features. And they talk and listen to manufacturers and vendors, some of whom are excellent kitesurfers in their own right and who can therefore talk with a degree of authority which inspires confidence.

There are other factors which impact on equipment selection, particularly when one comes from a related discipline such as windsurfing. The golden rule, however, is that each factor must be taken into account on a case-by-case basis. There is no such thing as the 'right' sailing, transport or storage equipment, other than the equipment that is right for you if you are to enjoy kitesurfing to the full.

Spoilt for choice.

The Quest for Self-Expression

Each year sees sales of some sixty thousand kiteboards worldwide, a high proportion of them sold to aficionados in France and Germany. Meanwhile, an organisation has been set up to regulate kitesurfing on a global basis: the International Kitesurfing Organisation (IKO). The sport is growing exponentially, with kitesurfers active on every continent: the year-on-year growth rate is estimated at around 30 per cent, an impressive statistic certainly, although kitesurfers continue to represent only a tiny community by comparison with other major sports disciplines. The number of kitesurf manufacturers is constantly increasing and new brands are appearing in the marketplace. There are also clear signs that the market is beginning to sort itself out. Equipment prices have shown a downward trend from 2004 and there is now a US discount house that has ruffled a few feathers amongst its competitors by offering heavily discounted prices and telesales facilities. The range of reasonably priced equipment on offer in the marketplace has increased significantly and devotees are now genuinely in a position to afford a sport that others in the past were obliged to give up for budgetary reasons.

Kitesurfing calls for a concerted mental and physical effort: Here, Étienne Lhote performs a backroll.

Kitesurfing Modes

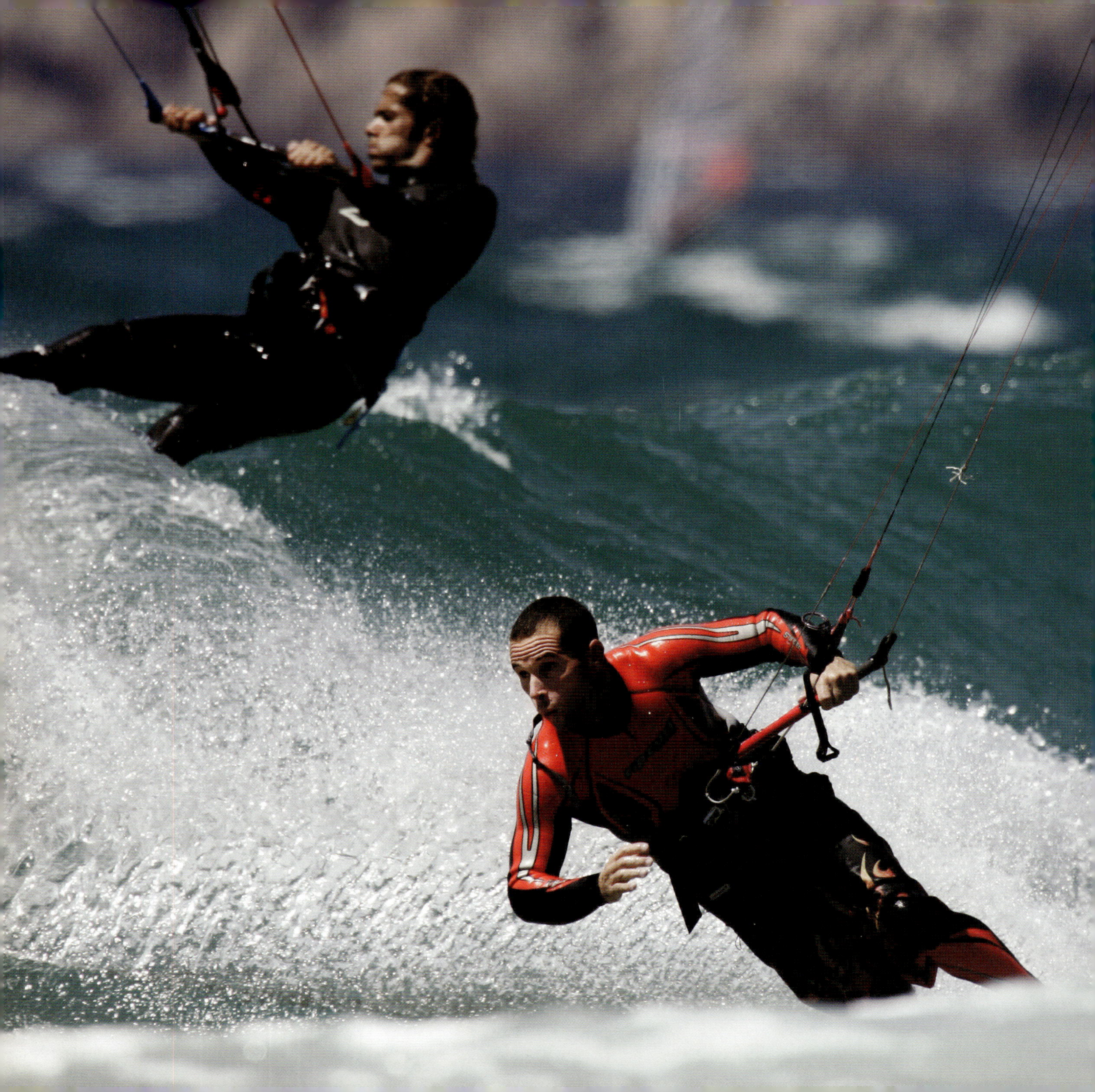

The emergence of various kitesurfing disciplines has resulted in the availability of equipment developed in conjunction with professionals, but in line with the expectations of part-timers. The various brands have had to adapt to accommodate demand. The media – and the specialist press in particular – have played their part by profiling kitesurfing and, by covering the sport's variants and options, have been instrumental in helping readers identify the style best suited to their own temperament and skill level. The kitesurfing public has also contributed by recommending as potential weekend or vacation destinations the various hotspots they themselves have visited around the world. Meanwhile, every kitesurfing mode and variant now has its own group of dedicated professionals who project a strong public image and boast an increasing level of expertise.

Freeriding and Tripping

What is the point of travelling to some almost deserted spot in some of the farthest-flung places in the world? And is all the physical effort, organisation, administration, transport and so on worth it to discover some spot miles from anywhere, where you and a couple of friends can indulge in some freeriding? (Make no mistake: freeriding all on your own is a definite no-no!) The answer may be that freeriding is a state of mind, a chance to get away from it all and indulge in uncomplicated and stress-free kitesurfing without a care in the world. It is a kitesurfing option that invokes an incomparable sense of inner peace in wide-open spaces, where you can ride free from constraint and without the need to be competitive. Better still, there is no need for strong winds; instead, you are at liberty to seek out a beautiful lagoon or a magnificent stretch of beach and simply let time stand still.

Above: *Kitesurfing is tailor-made for wide-open spaces and nature-lovers.*

Left-hand page: *A magnificent playground.*

Above *Mum's the word! Soaring at will above the turquoise waters of Fiji.*

Right-hand page: *Kitesurfing in Essaoura, historical gateway to the North African desert: Rachid Roussafi surfs near Mogador.*

Freeriding is an option open to the vast majority of kitesurfers and it is a mode they generally regard as the most uplifting, with extended runs which give free rein to the surfer's imagination and to his or her capacity to take in the beauty of the surroundings. This is not to say that tricks and jumps cannot be thrown in to break the monotony of straight-line runs; far from it, they can be interspersed at will whenever you feel like it. Inevitably perhaps, specialist tour operators have seized on freeriding to promote dream vacation destinations and kitesurfers have duly flocked there, anxious to visit places the pros endorse in holiday brochures. Those first intrepid travellers have revelled in the opportunity to experience, relive, analyse and cherish those very special kitesurfing moments. Be warned, however: it's best to book now, before it's too late …

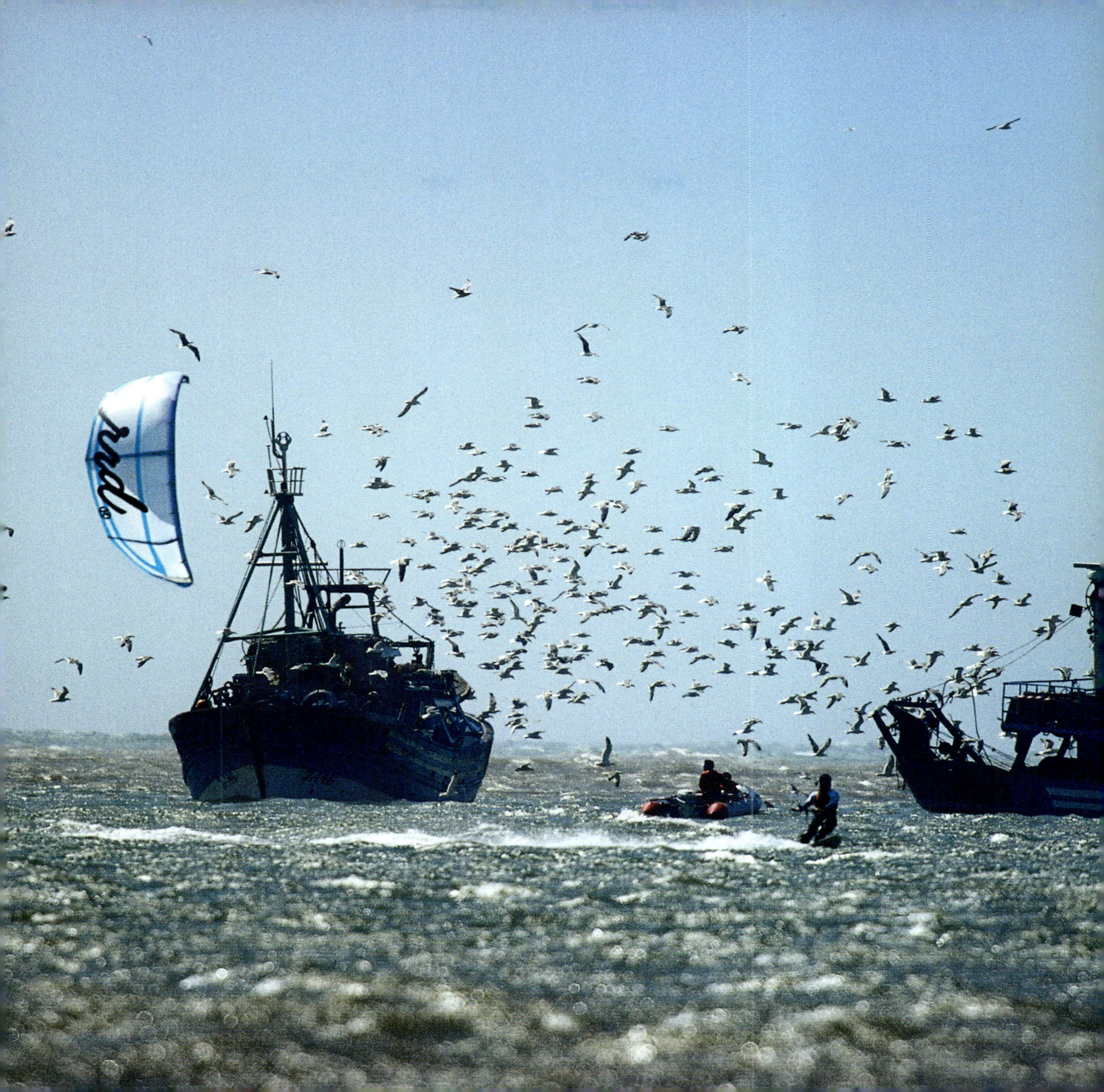
rrd

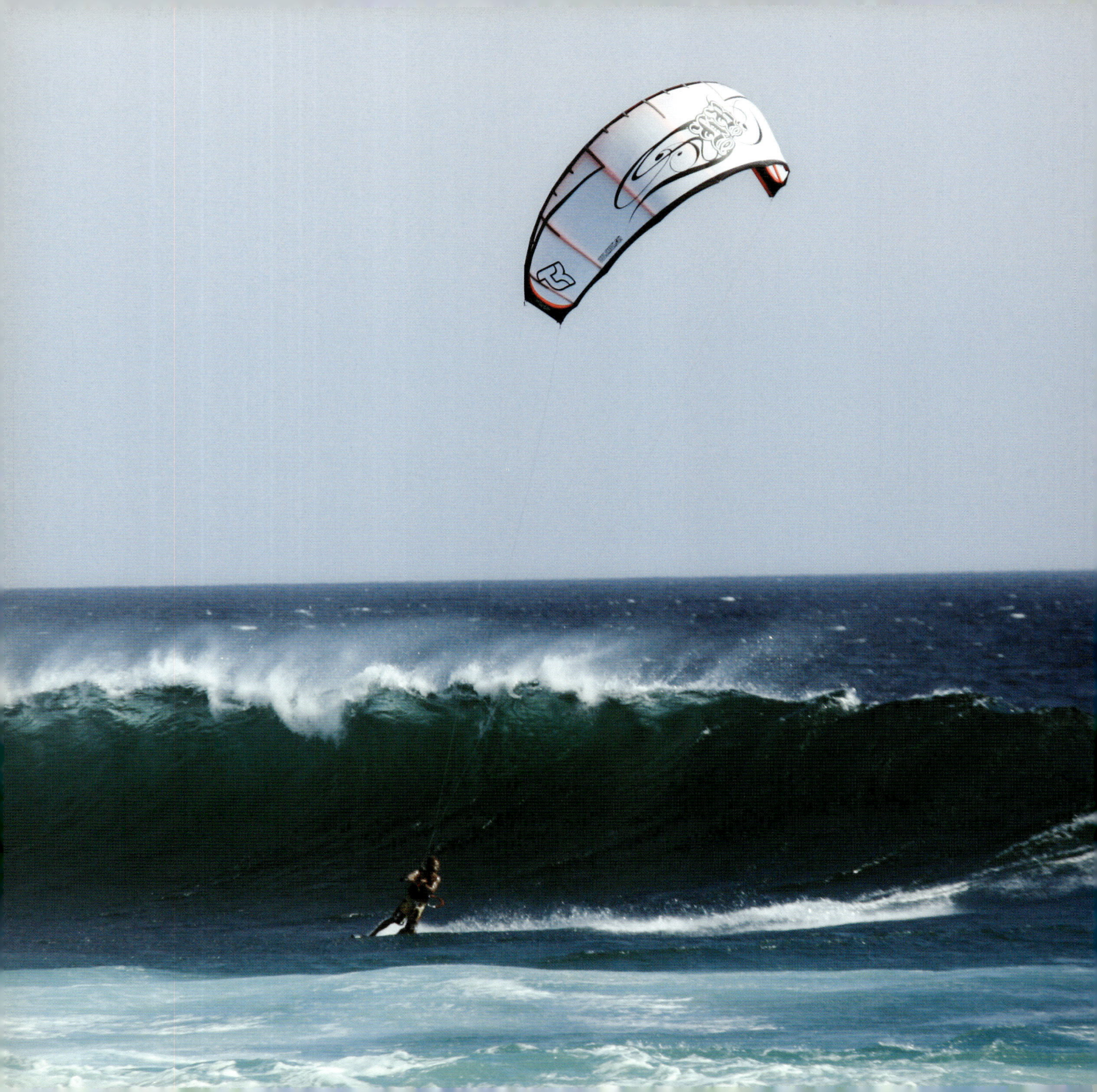

Surf and Wave

Surfing has inspired generation after generation of water-sports fanatics and it still remains unique in terms of its purity and the close bond it creates between the surfer and his or her element, the ocean. The irrepressible urge to ride the waves cuts across every surfing discipline. For some, it is an end in itself, a religion almost. They rely on the waves to generate the energy needed to execute their moves and perform their stunts. And, in time, they shift up a gear or two, riding progressively higher and more powerful waves until one day perhaps – and this is surely every surfer's dream – they make it into the hallowed 'green room', the ultimate challenge and the Holy Grail to which only the very best can aspire. Who could ever have imagined that a kitesurfer trailing 25 to 30 metres of lines might one day dare to enter The Tube? No one. Yet it has been done, establishing beyond doubt that kitesurfing has no apparent limits. In kitesurfing, it seems, everything is possible, however extreme. The expert kitesurfer is constantly looking for new challenges, constantly travelling down new and unexplored paths, scouring the globe for new hotspots and optimal water and weather conditions. The breakthrough came in Mauritius and Indonesia in 2004 when a tiny group of seasoned kitesurfers decided to go for it. They deliberately launched themselves into The Tube. And their wildest dreams became reality. Their exploit was the culmination of a seven-year dream that, one day, they would invade the sanctity of The Tube. Suddenly, the myth had been exploded. As the news flashed around the kitesurfing world, heads shook in admiration and disbelief. Kitesurfing was a comparatively young discipline, but it had demonstrated yet again its capacity for continuous innovation, its ability to reinvent itself on an ongoing basis. There was only one question on everyone's lips: What next?

The quest for the wave remains eternal. Here, Hervé Bouré.

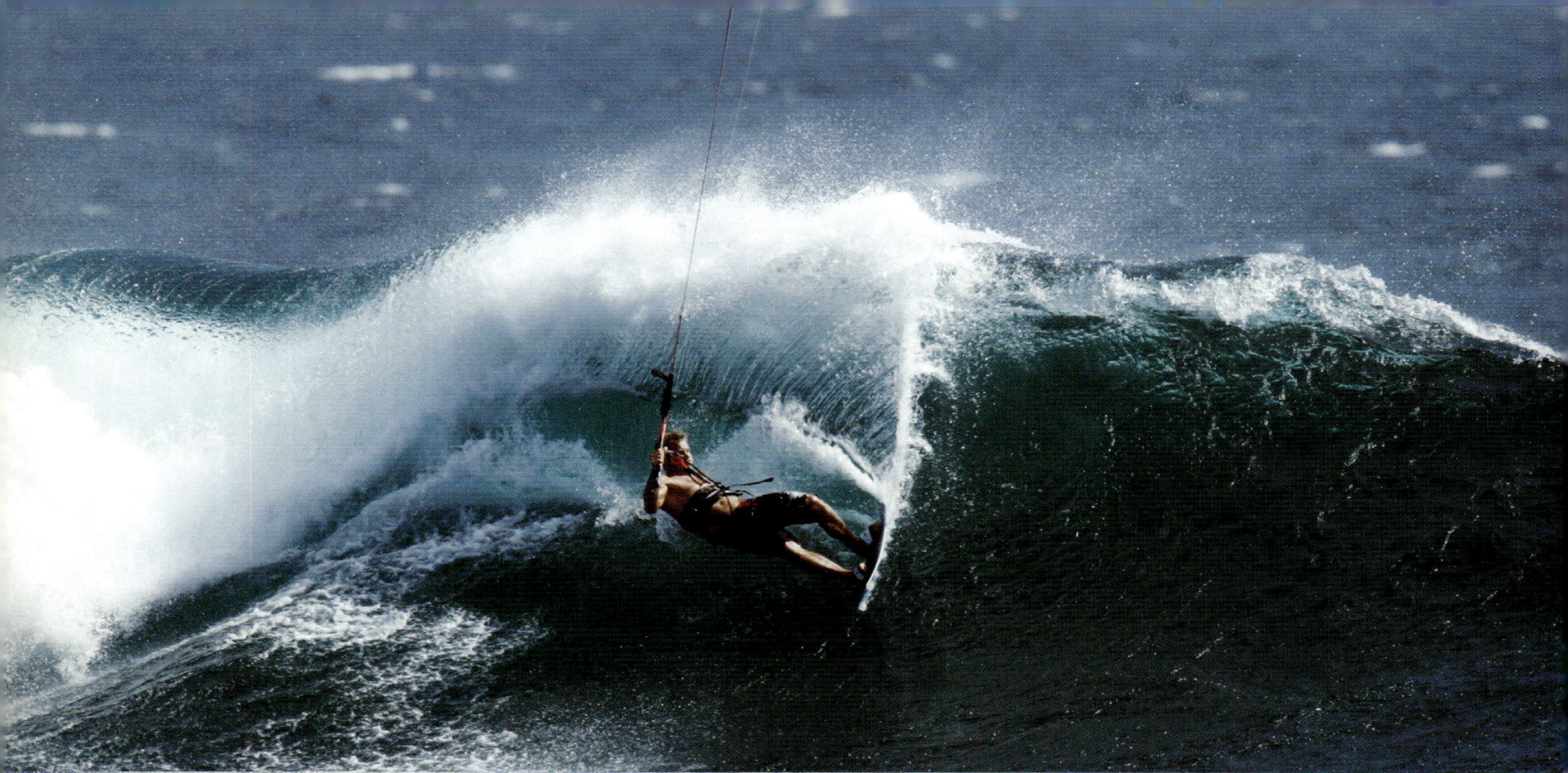

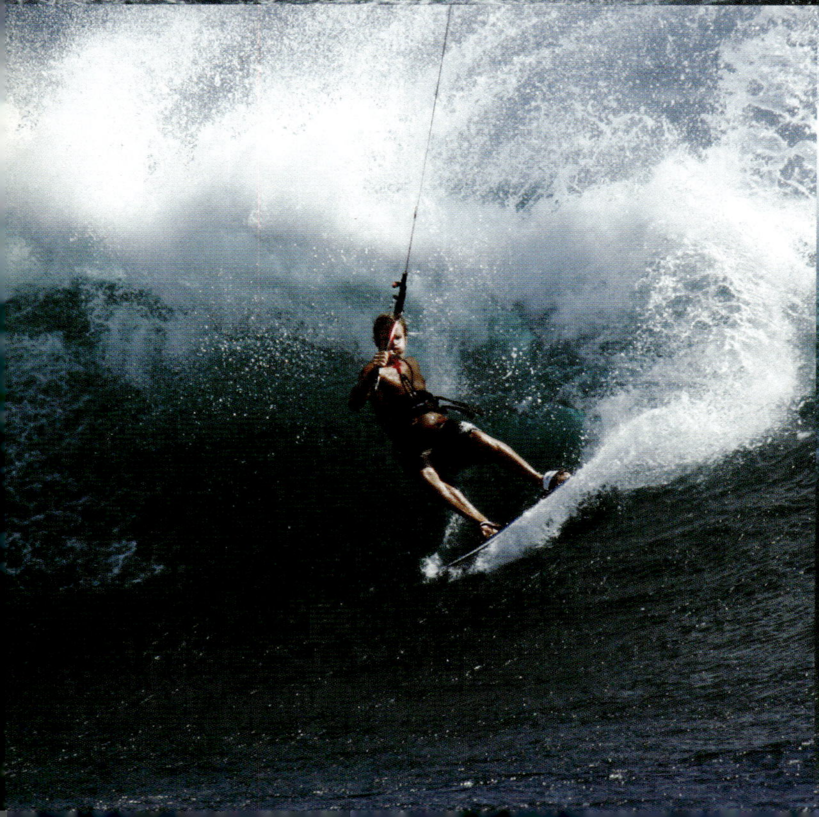

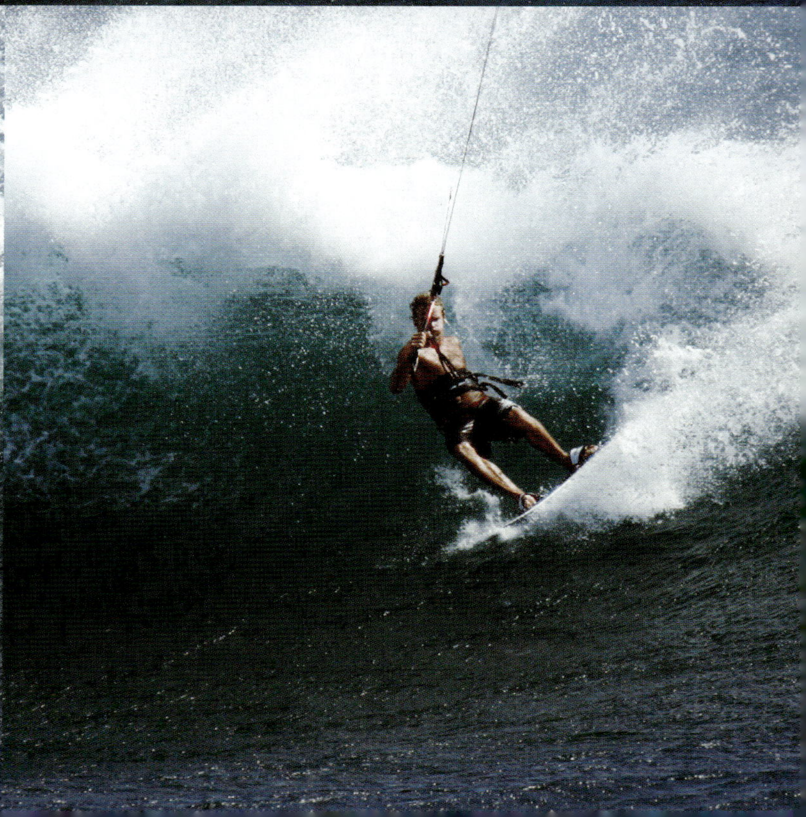

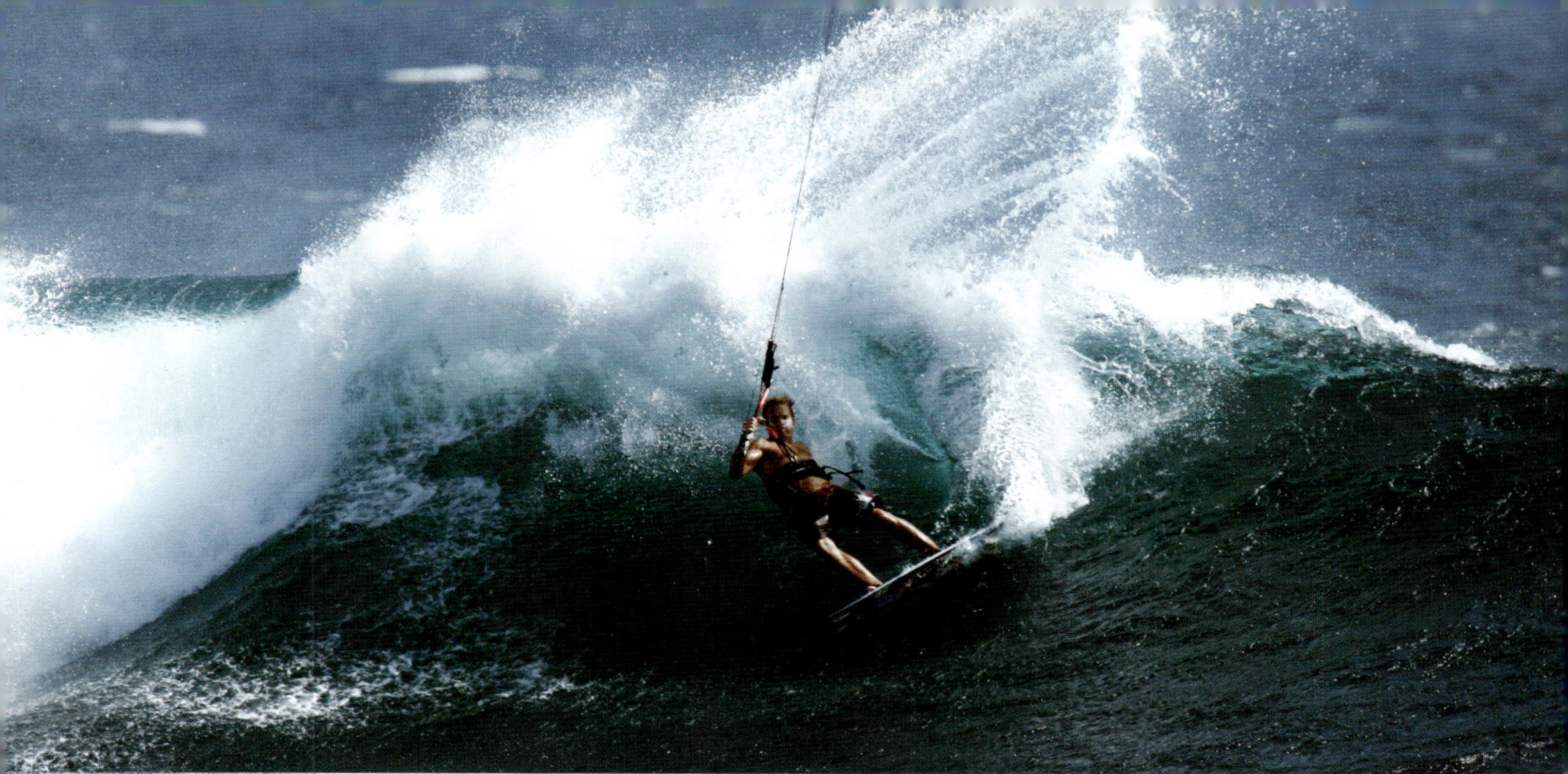
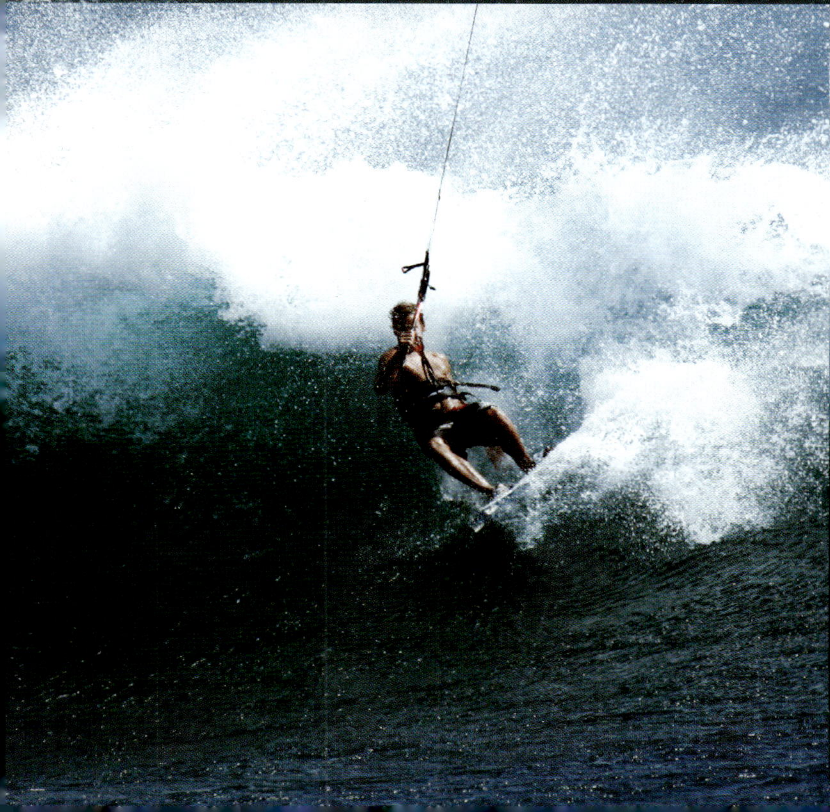
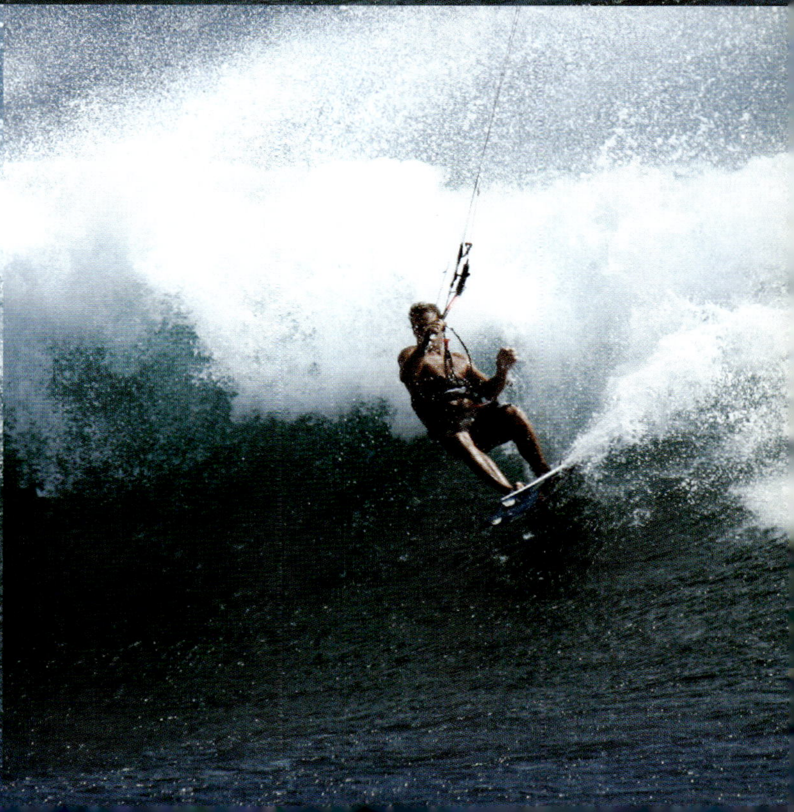

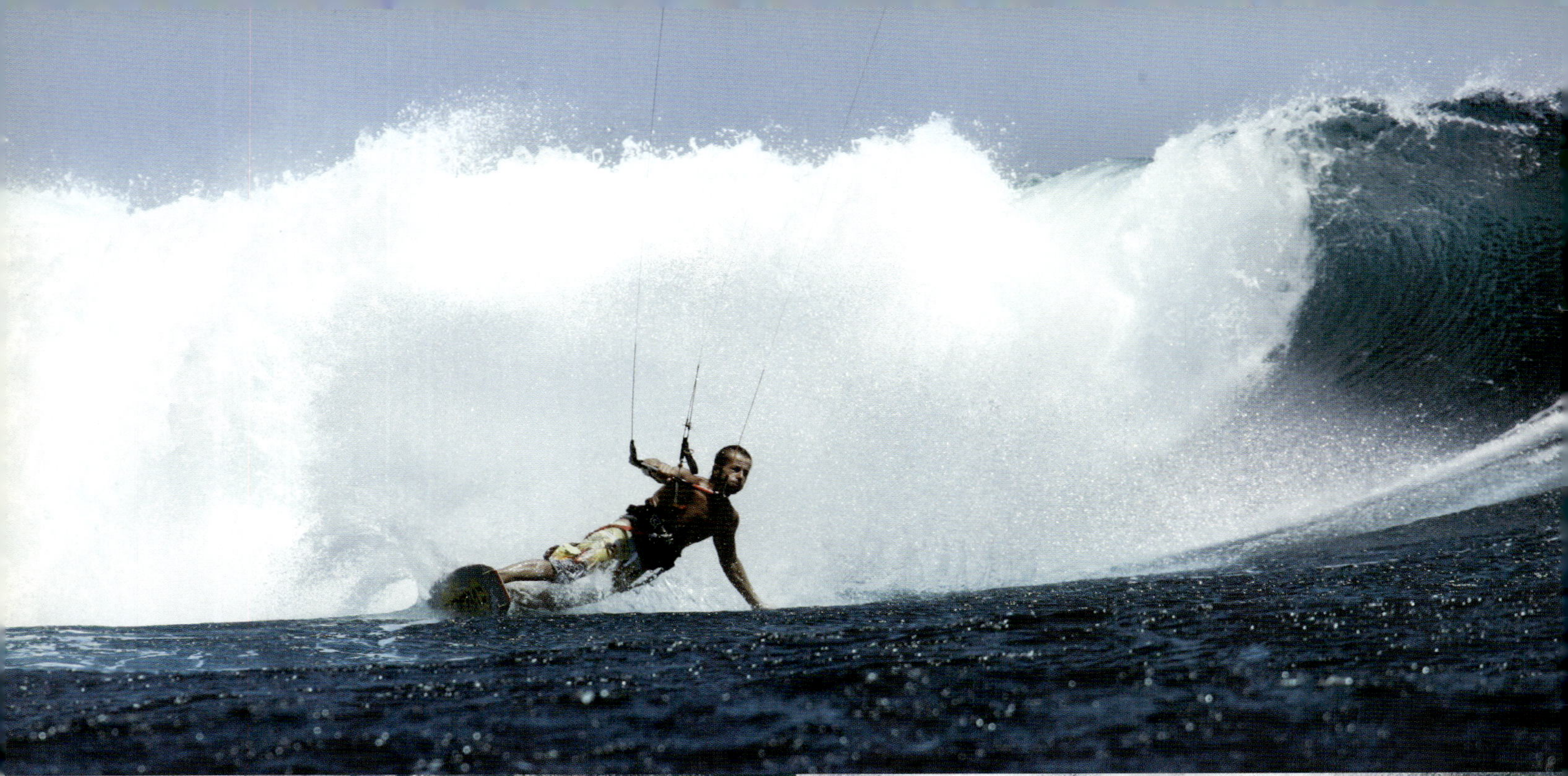
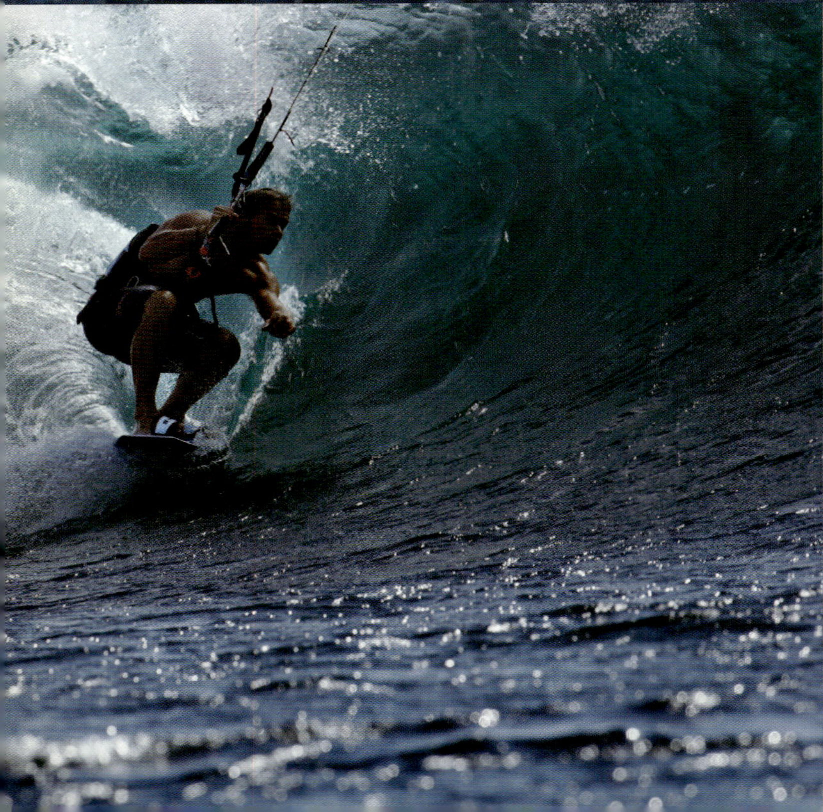
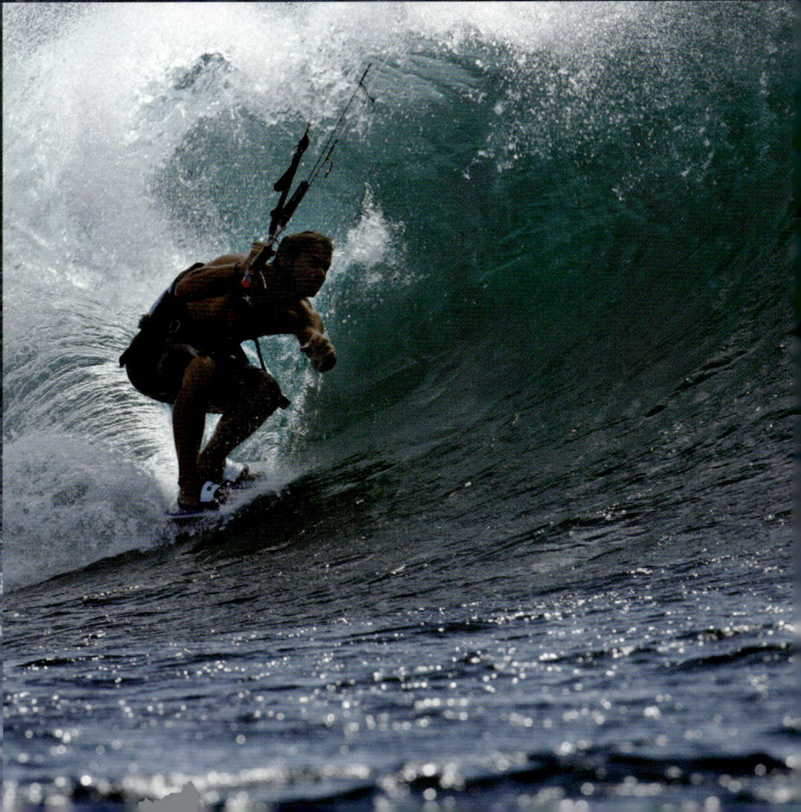

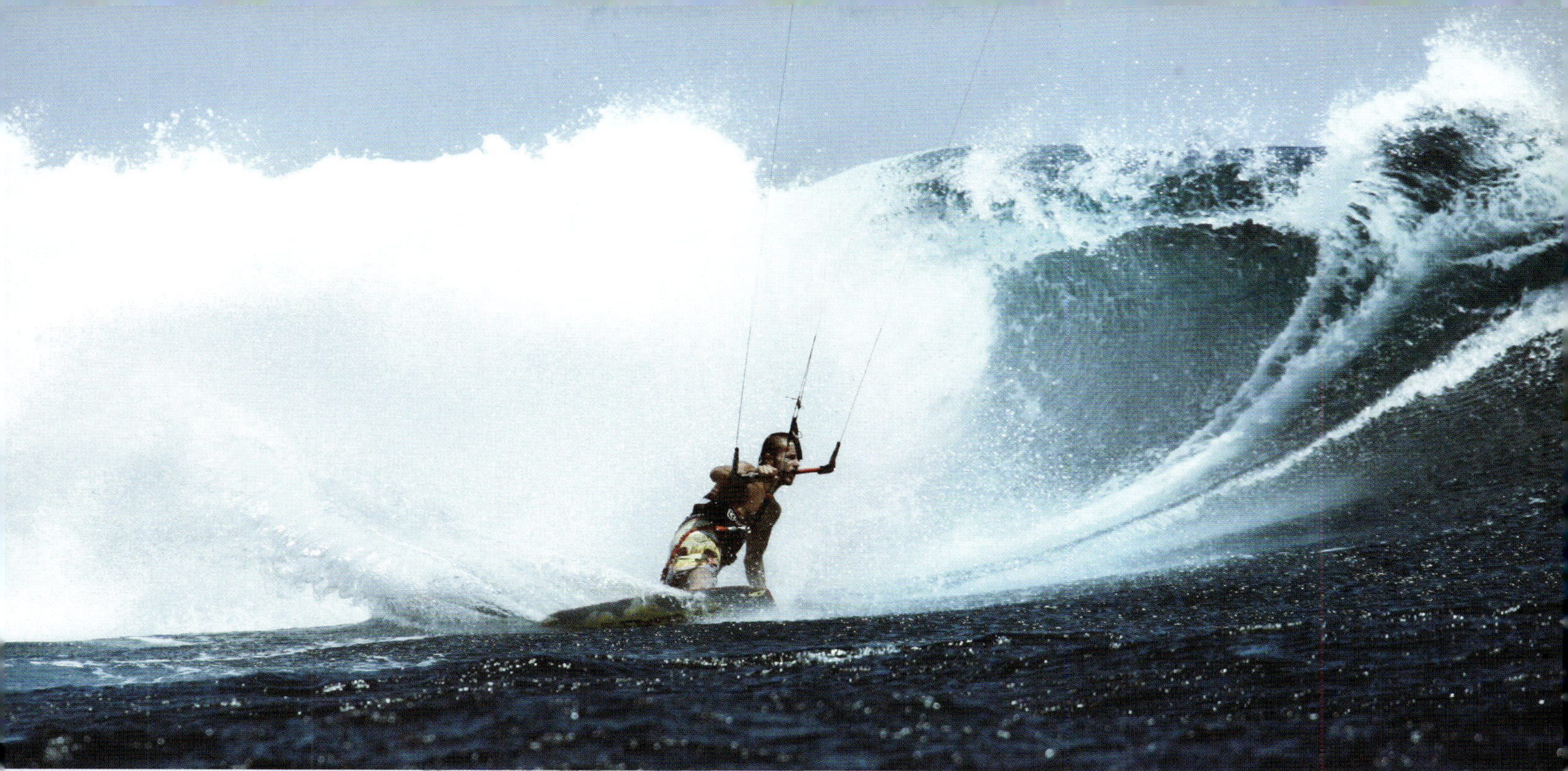
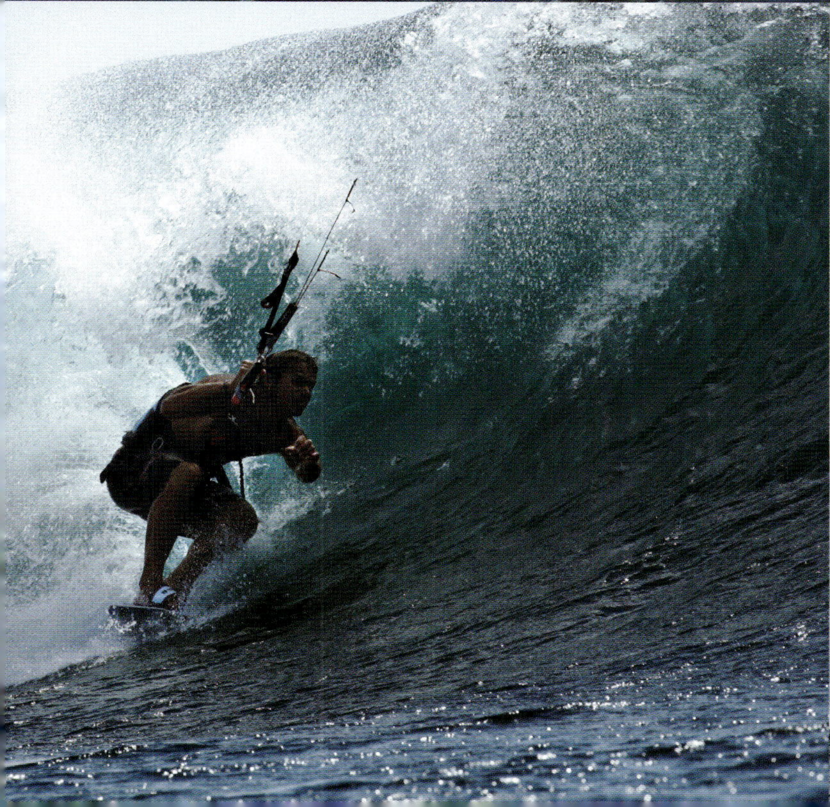
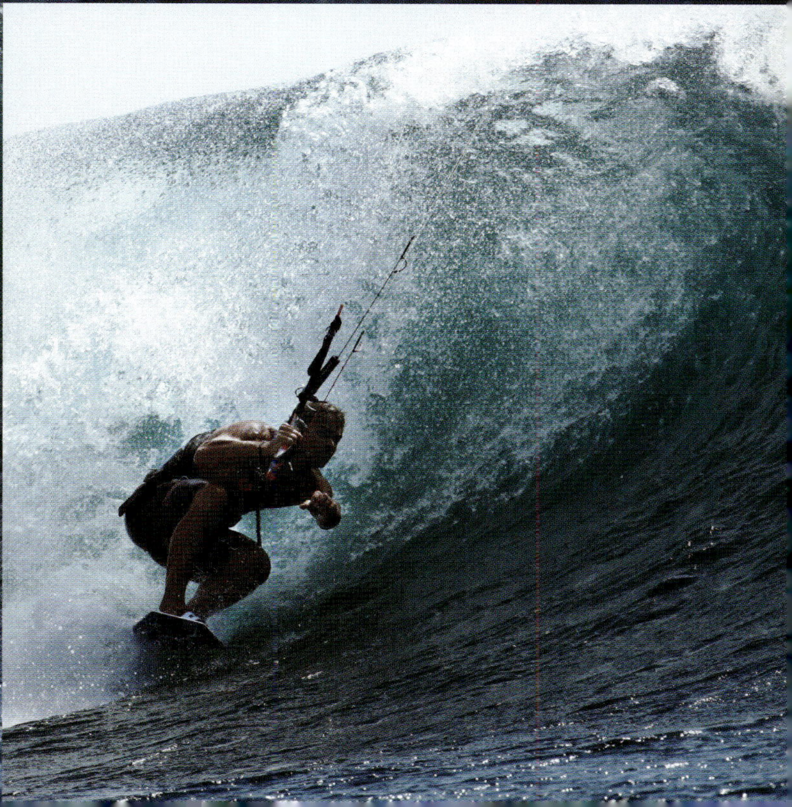

Wakeboard

Watching riders who adopt a wakeboard approach to kitesurfing tends to be like watching a group of boisterous kids clowning around on the water and in the air. The wakeboard mode carries over distinctive features from wakeboarding proper: fixed footholds that facilitate moves and tricks, a wider and thinner reinforced board with smaller fins or no fins whatsoever, a two- or four-line kite, a truncated control bar a bit like a wakeboard rudder, and a safety leash that tends to get in the way of rotations. What all this paraphernalia adds up to is a piece of tackle that announces the wakeboard kitesurfer's 'radical' intentions and his or her commitment to a highly personal approach and style.

Wakeboarding originated in the United States and wakeboard kitesurfing came into its own in Maui, Hawaii, where Lou Wainman and Eliot Leboe have posted new benchmarks. These two are still without peers, although there are a number of challengers and aficionados waiting in the wings, notably erstwhile skaters, snowboarders and wakeboarders who have been bitten by the kitesurfing bug. The wakeboard mode has added a new dimension to kitesurfing and promises to develop as an important branch of the sport.

Acrobatics virtuoso André Philip goes for an aggressive Indy-grab (opposite) *and a tail-grab* (right-hand page, left).

Right-hand page, right: *The whole body is involved in this style of manœuvre; powerful inverse tail grab by Teiva Joyeux.*

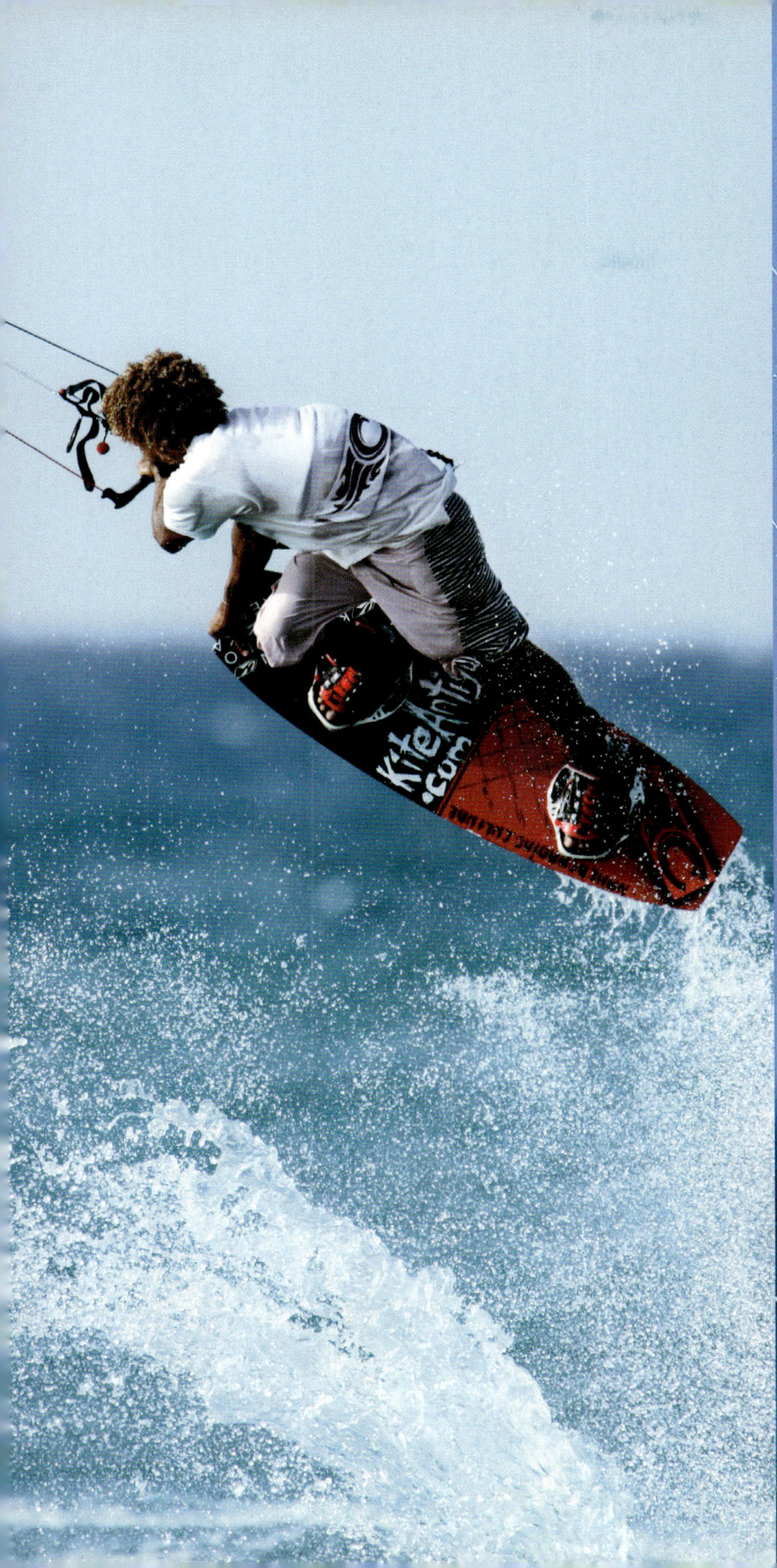
KiteAntics.com
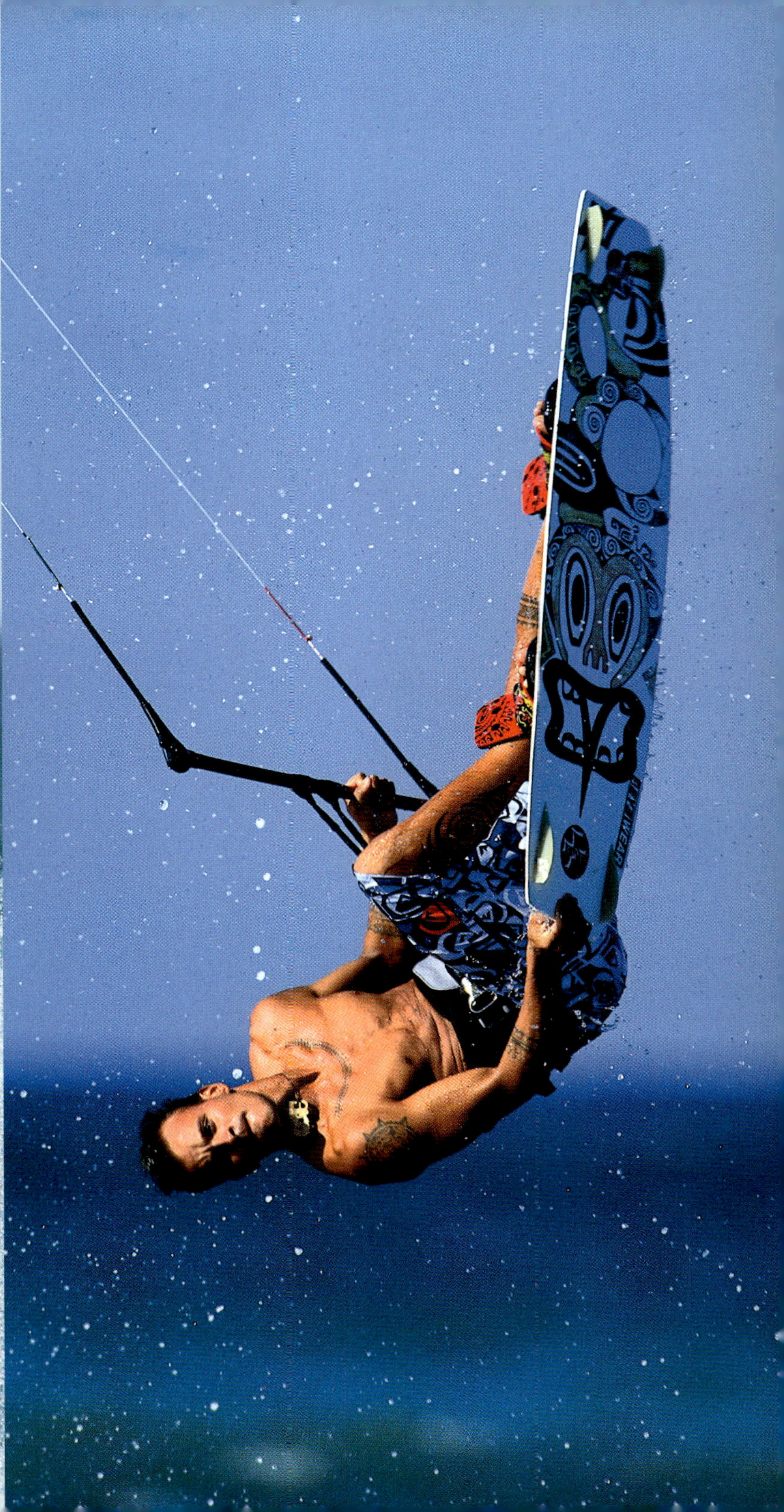

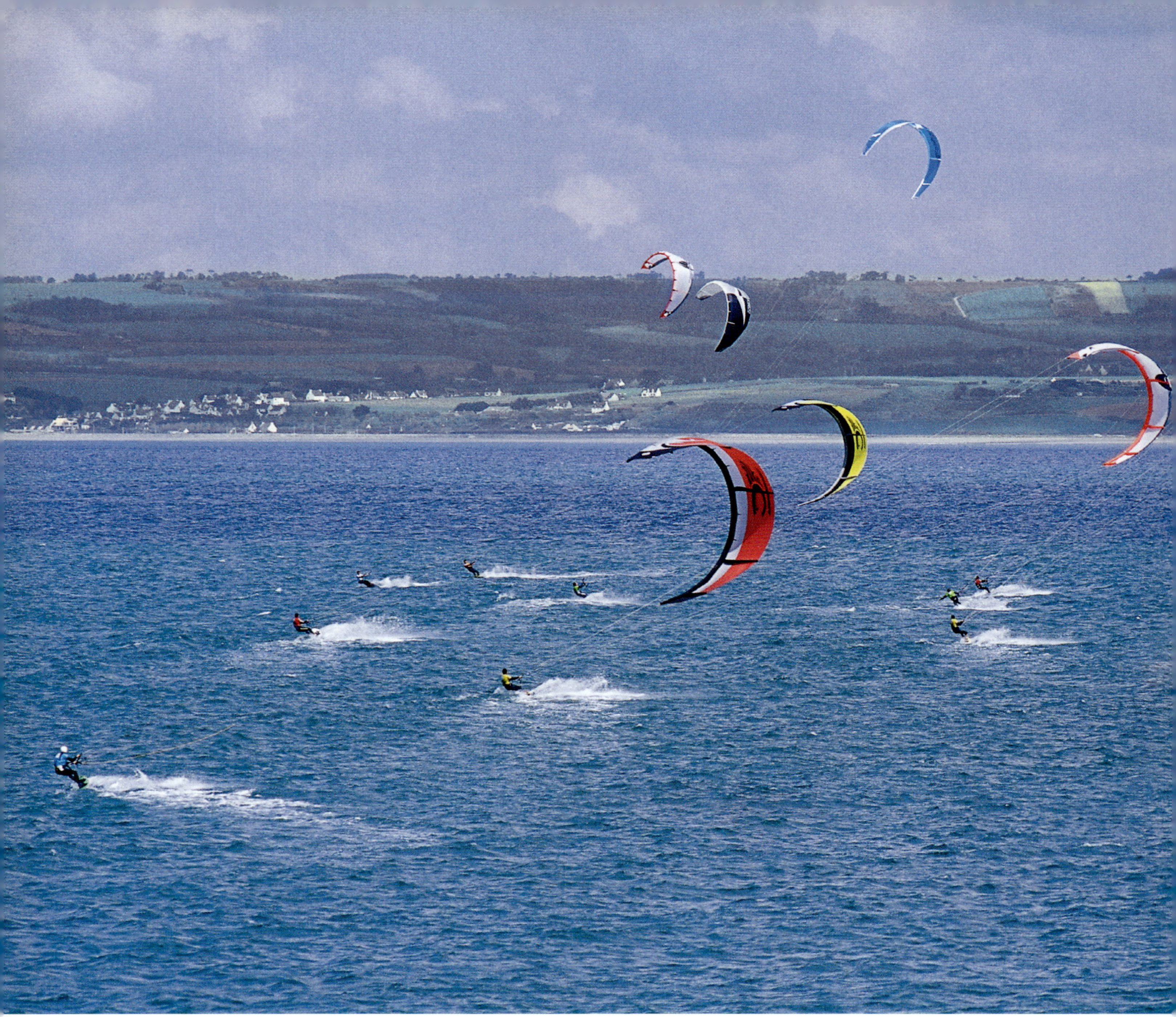

Speed Crossing

As a kitesurfing discipline, speed crossing owes a considerable debt to windsurfing. This extreme mode now enjoys increasing popularity among both professionals and part-timers and is a darling of the media. Back in the earliest days of kitesurfing, Manu Bertin ploughed a lone furrow as a one-off pioneer of crossings in the Hawaiian archipelago, off Greenland and, latterly, in the English Channel between the island of Batz (Brittany) and The Lizard (Cornwall). His early exploits fired the public imagination and put the media on alert.

The impressive spectacle of kites setting out to sea *en masse* has proved a major factor in promoting the speed crossing mode generally and attracting new converts. Speed crossing is now a media event and organisers of watersport-events have been quick to latch on to its potential. The 2002 Grand Prix Petit Navire regatta in Dourdnenez, Brittany, for example, introduced a first-ever kitesurfing event alongside its traditional and increasingly popular Dragon Class and windsurfing categories. Of late, there has been a rapid proliferation of official speed crossing events, among them competitions in France, Turkey, New Caledonia, England and New Zealand. Kitesurfing has come of age not only as a sport but, it would seem, as a spectacle.

Speed-crossing competitions are a grandiose spectacle for competitors, onlookers and media alike.

Full speed ahead for a hair-raising run …

Speed Racing

Every individual sports discipline will, sooner or later, generate competition, as a result of a deep-down and atavistic drive to measure one's own performance against that of others. Speed racing is no exception to this unwritten rule and, unlike other kitesurfing options and variants, it is a discipline governed by a performance evaluation system that is both impartial and infallible. Individual runs over a 500-metre course are timed by means of photo-cell chronometry calibrated to a world standard. The approach is ruggedly instrument-based and no provision is made for subjective marking. There is no place for value judgement or human error: the clock decides. It follows that the pressure is enormous. Contestants taking to the water and coming up to the start line watch their rivals going through their pre-race routine. The atmosphere is electric, all the more so since the action takes place close to the shore. The kiters look for a calm stretch of water, dependent on the offshore wind that frequently affects these events. Speed and downforce are dictated by customised board configurations. Competitors put on as much kite sail as they can handle in the hope that a sudden gust of wind will boost their speed and give them the extra edge needed to carry the day. Their bodies are honed by sessions in the gym, fine-tuned to withstand the powerful onrush of wind. They wear weighted vests as ballast. Men and women start on an equal footing, the former jostling for a front-line position, the latter forcing their way in as best they can. As they make their approach, however, no physical interference is allowed. The spectators on the shore sense the tension building. The God of Winds sits in judgement … The current all-category record was posted in the summer of 2004 by Manu Taub: 40.58 knots – beating his own record time set that spring at the Mondial du Vent world wind championships held in Leucate.

A study in contrasts: After a taxing run against the clock, it's time to make one's way back to the starting position. This time, Cory Roesler has elected to walk.

Freestyle

Freestyle is universally acknowledged as the benchmark competition technique. Riders spend days and weeks on end practising takeoffs as a prelude to moves that range from Big Air jumps to complex midair figures. They also practise landings, because these are also scored. Freestyle is spectacular because the keynote is variety. The idea is to impress the judges with a repertoire of figures that are unique to the individual kitesurfer, including linked sequences comprising a permutation of quick-fire tricks and other, more ample, sequences that can be savoured at leisure. Figures are single or combination – tail grab, s-bend, handle pass, backroll, pitrose, tantrum, double front board-off, double board-off fin grab – each calculated to make their mark with the jury.

Freestyle is an extraordinary discipline. It derives much of its charm and fascination from knife-edge uncertainty, from anticipation that a rider may pull a move off or come a cropper in the process, from the sheer disbelief in watching the well-nigh impossible manoeuvres executed by rider and kite. For the novice, the sight of these professionals at work is, on the one hand, compulsive and a far cry from day-to-day kitesurfing and, on the other, an inspiration: what would the beginner give to perform the merest fraction of these stunning moves?

Freestyle, as the name implies, is the freest of kitesurfing disciplines in the sense that individual riders are at liberty to express themselves by giving free rein to their imagination, subject only to the limits of their own technique and skill. Freestyle surprises and seduces. Its acrobatic dimension is a media magnet, epitomising the dynamism, energy, vitality and athleticism of youth.

Opposite: *Nothing is more fun than freestyle: Charles Deleau plays Icarus as he executes a front-no-foot tail-grab.*

Double-page spread overleaf: *Étienne Lhote completely airborne during a Moebius backroll.*

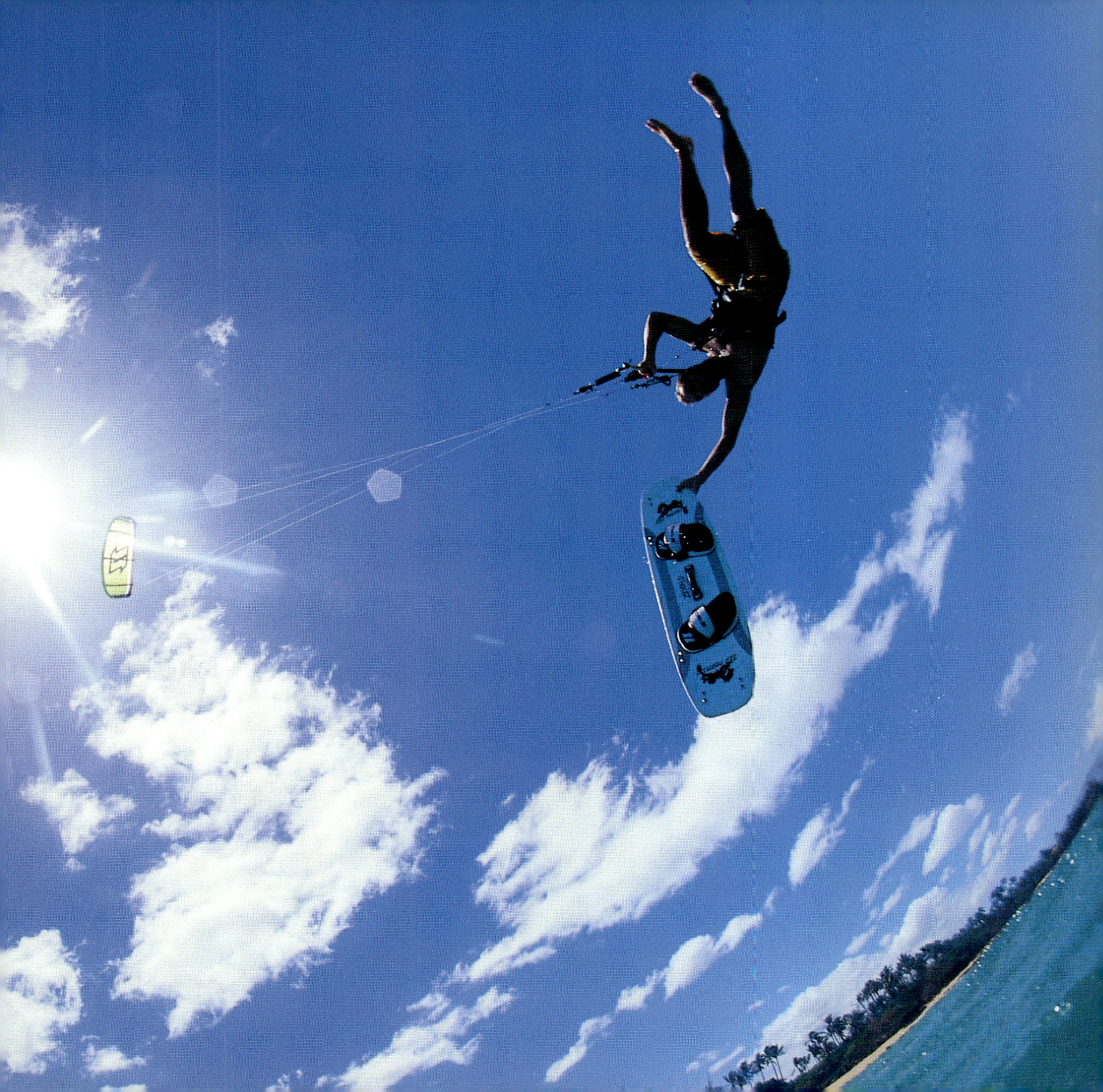

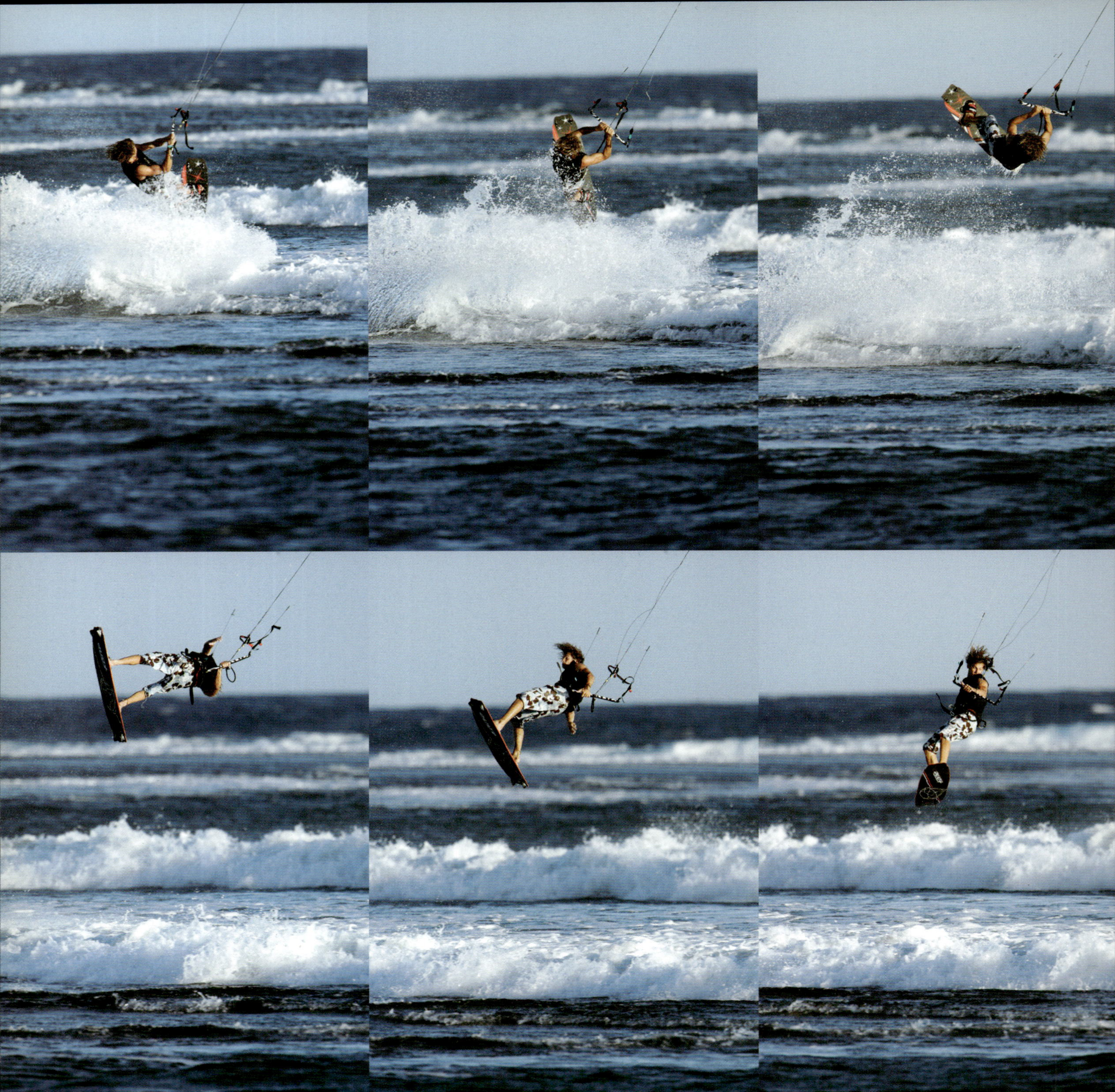

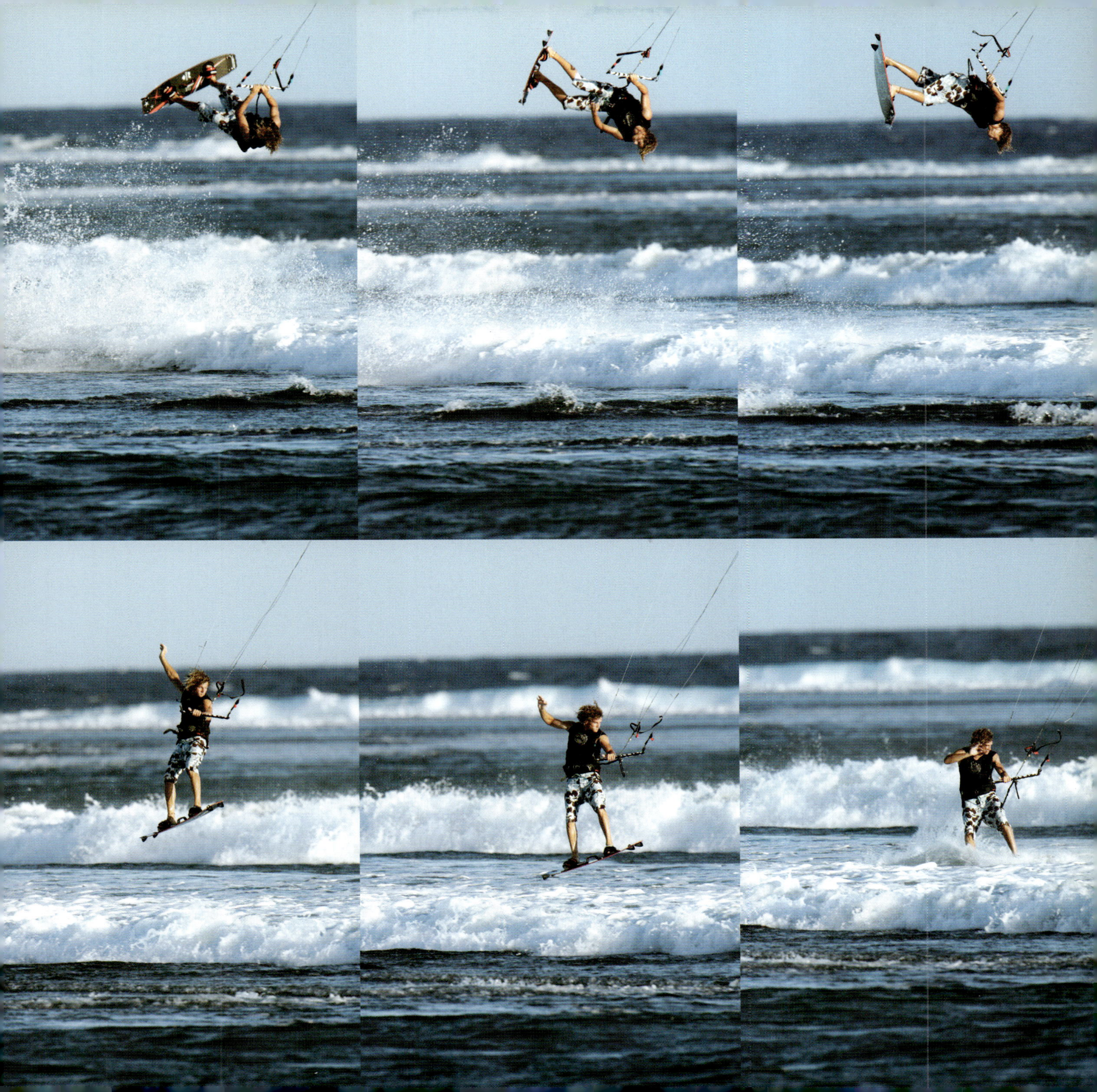

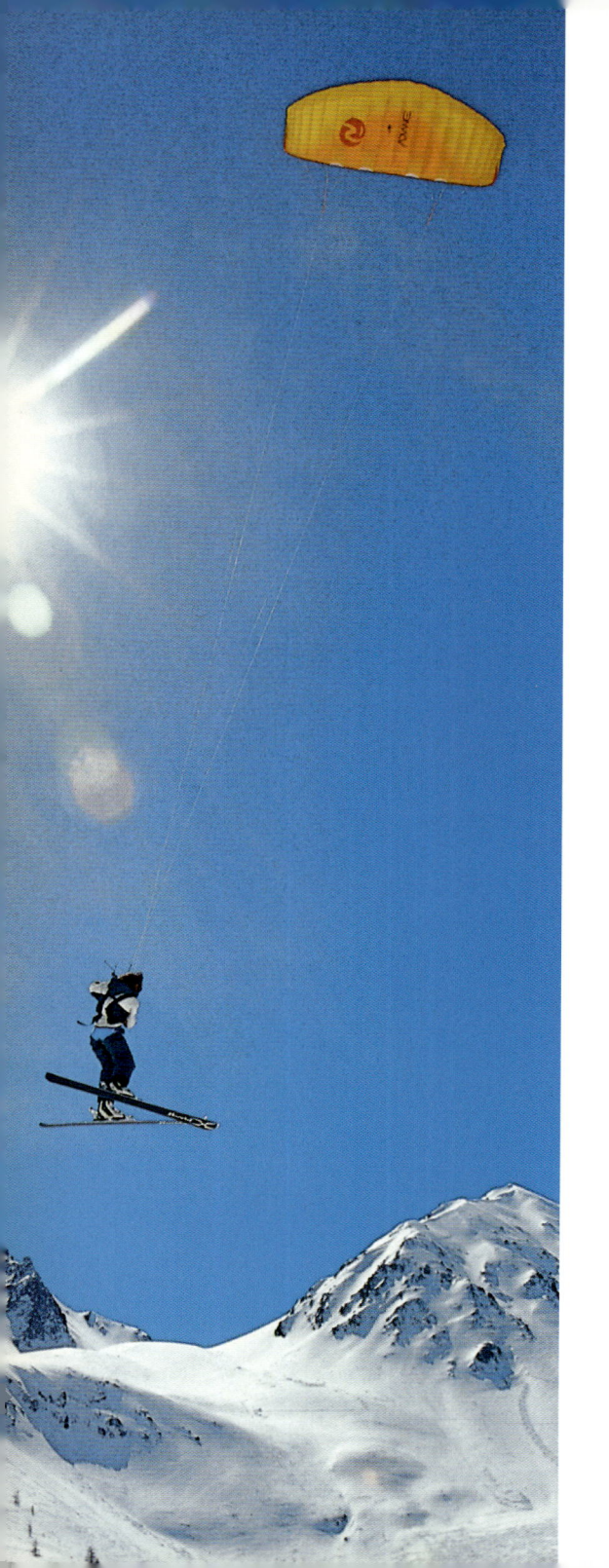

Snowkiting

Of all kitesurfing derivatives such as mountain board or kite buggy, snowkiting is probably the most extraordinary. It is an extension of its close cousins skiing and kitesurfing, and, like kitesurfers the world over, snowkiters have come to realise that this variant affords them a heightened degree of freedom, in this instance on otherwise inaccessible mountain peaks and interminably flat tracts of snow in the far north. With a kite, they are free to surf the mountainsides and the windswept plains and take to the air even more spectacularly – if that were possible – than from the water. At times, the snowkiter will take to the air for distances that would do credit to a paraglider.

The snowkiting variant appeared some five years ago but already boasts its own world championship which, in 2004, comprised four events in France, the United States, Norway and Switzerland. The media, ever anxious to highlight a new fad, has taken to snowkiting with a vengeance, and initial sponsorship interest has already ensured that this young discipline is poised to gain new adherents and expand exponentially.

Opposite and right-hand page: *A family atmosphere: Big-air for Pascal Joubert* (left) *and an off-the-lip for Guillaume Chastagnol* (right).

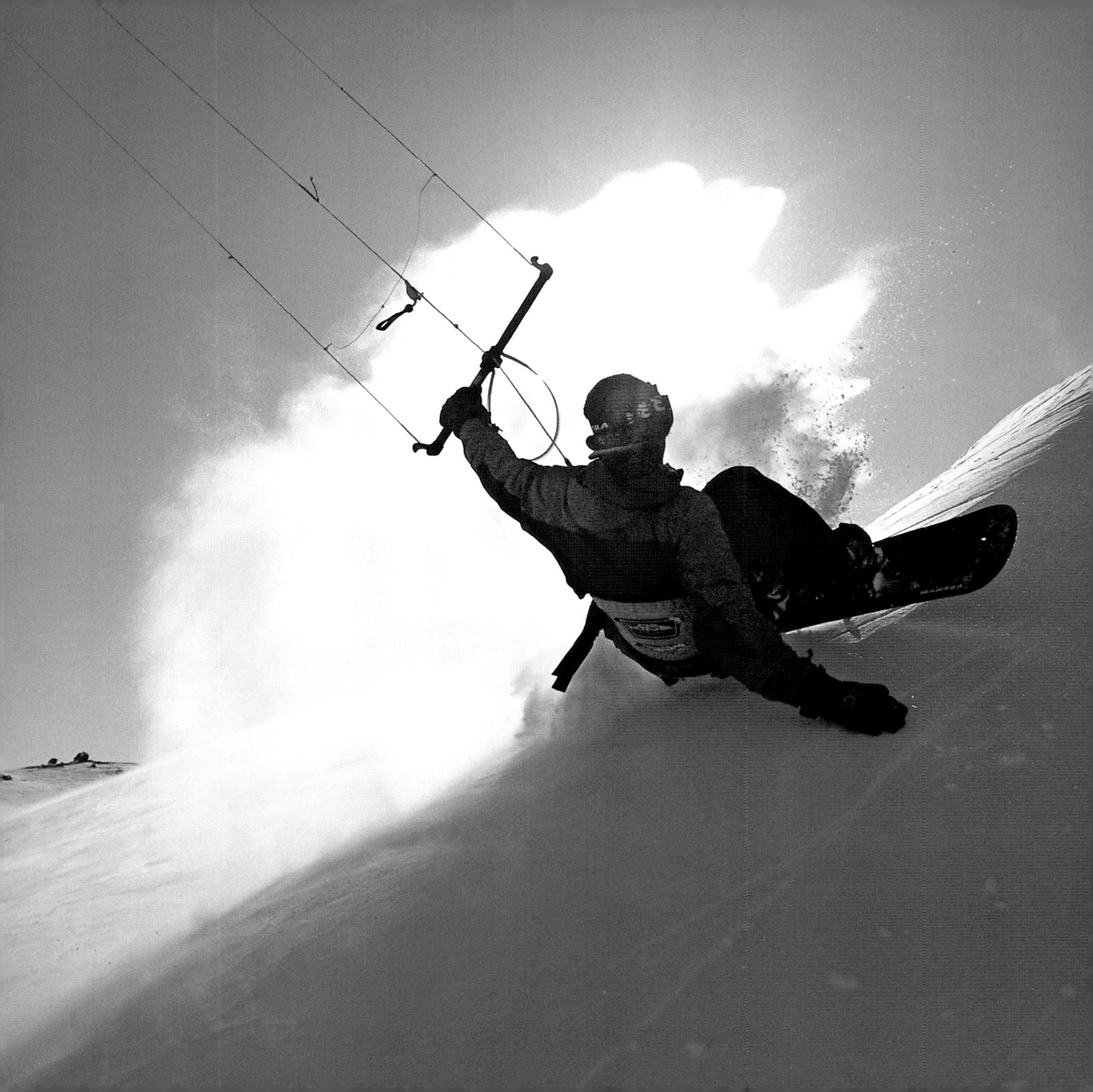

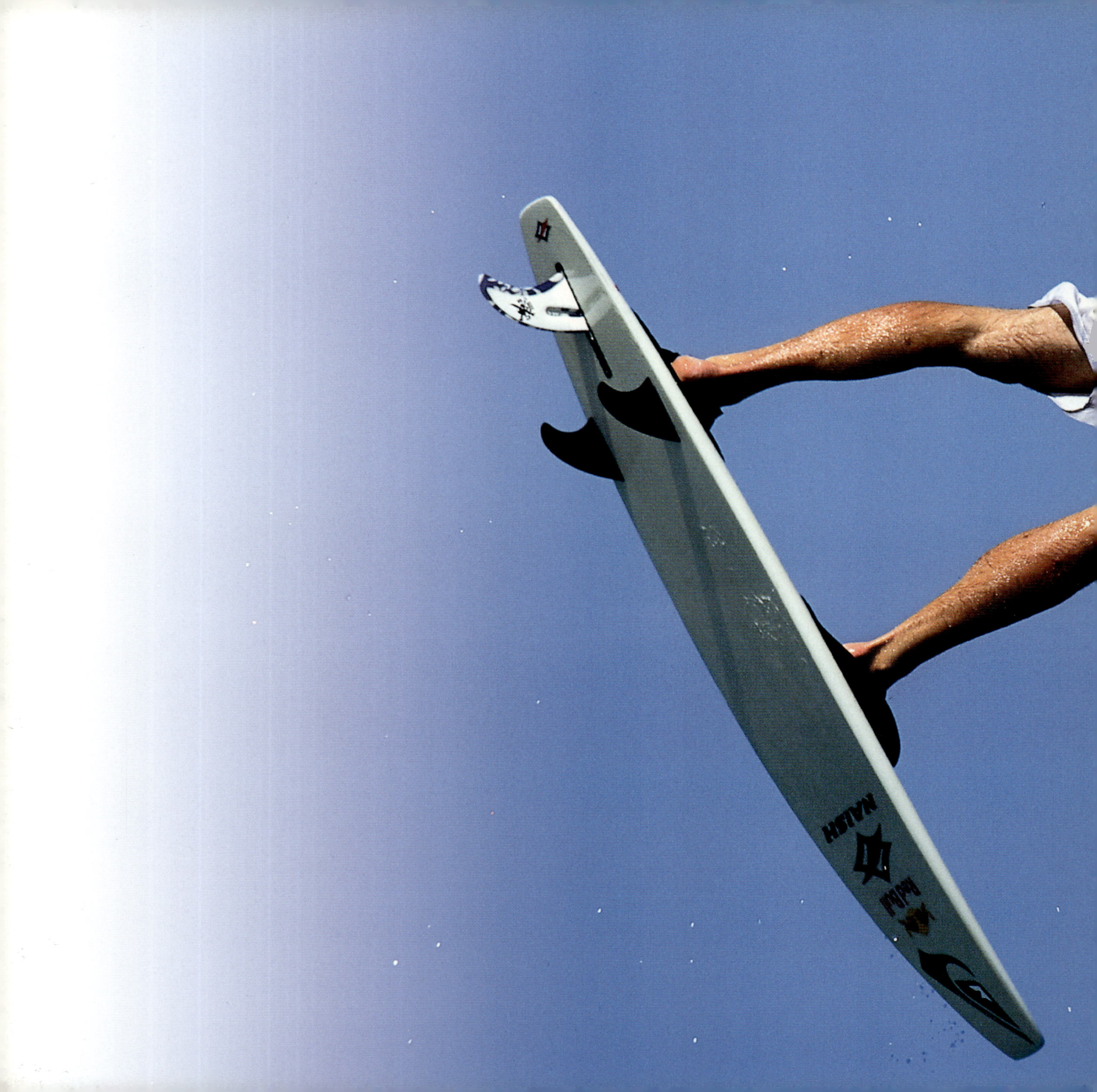
NAISH

Kitesurfing Icons

Naish
robby

Legend and King

Robby Naish was born in La Jolla, California in 1963 and has lived in Hawaii since his early teens. Naish is the benchmark performer, his name a byword in surfing myth and legend. A world champion windsurfer at the tender age of thirteen, Robby went on to rack up title after title. Beginning in 1976, he chalked up in excess of 25 world windsurfing championship firsts. He is now acknowledged as one of the founding fathers and pioneers of both windsurfing and kitesurfing and, to this day, he is still a top-level performer in both disciplines. He posted the kitesurfing world speed record in 2002 and the world hangtime record, set at the Red Bull King of the Air Contest of 2003.

This incredible slate of titles and records has already made Naish into arguably the world's most celebrated waterman, but, for all that, he is always on the lookout for fresh challenges. There is nothing new in this: back in the 1990s, as supremo of windsurfing equipment manufacturer Naish Sails and one of the key figures in the surfing industry alongside Kelly Slater, it was Robby who checked out the embryonic phase of kitesurfing in the skies over Hawaii. Naish might have been tempted to rest on his reputation and his laurels in the windsurfing industry, not to mention his class and innate charisma, but that was not his style. Instead, he launched himself full-tilt into the kitesurfing industry, immediately recognising its potential. He started making kites and boards and, today, Naish Kiteboarding is the number-two brand worldwide behind Wipeka. His inflatable kite technology, developed under licence from the Legaignoux brothers, is the global market leader in terms of sales.

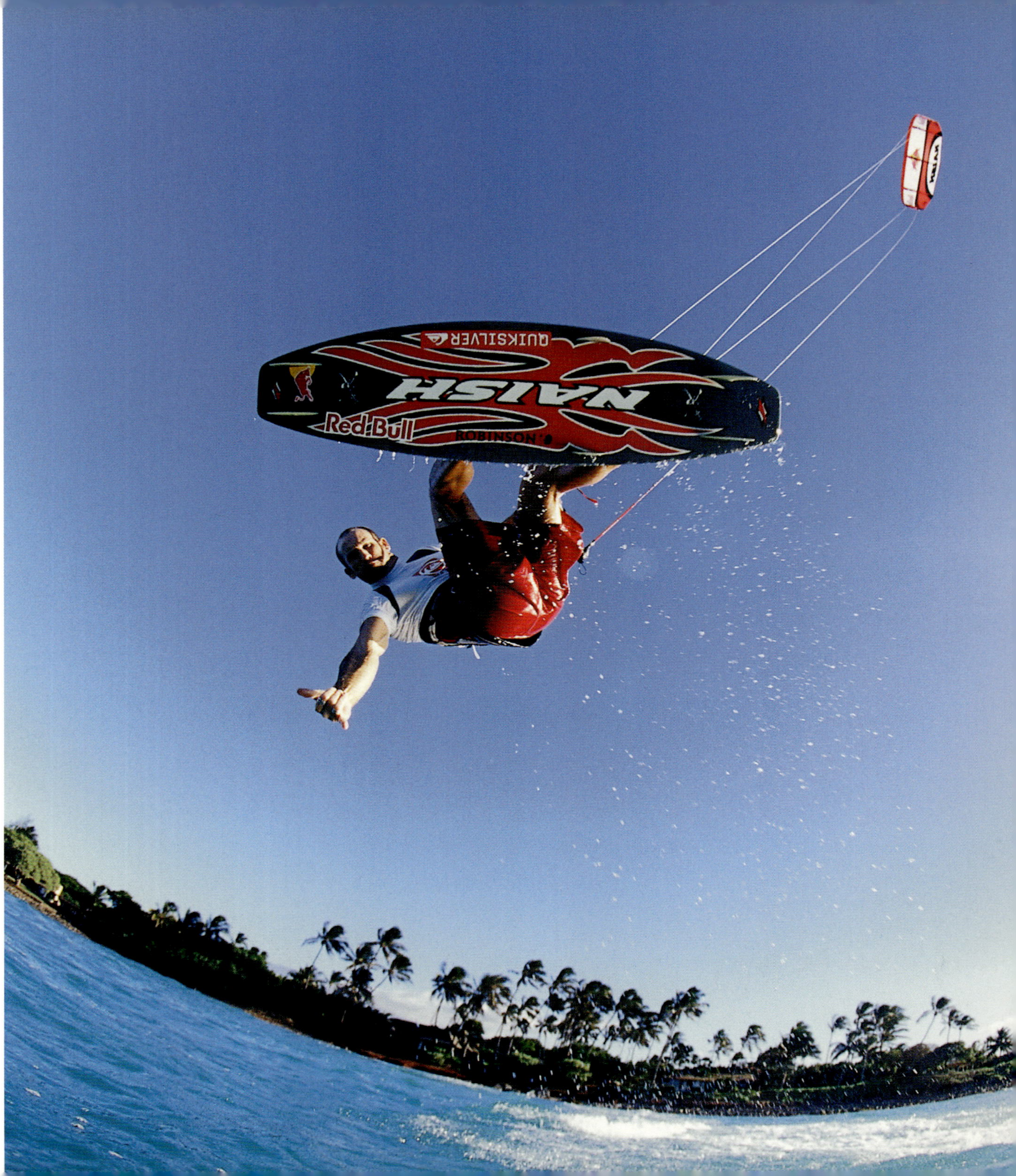
QUIKSILVER
NAISH
Red Bull
ROBINSON

Among Robby Naish's multifarious talents is a visionary entrepreneurial skill that enabled him to steer his company through the vagaries of an untried yet expanding market. Naish led the way and others followed.

Robby Naish is beyond any doubt a kitesurfing legend whose influence on the sport has been global. His creativity and marketing know-how have combined to develop the celebrated Naish Wave Party event. One of his other great strengths, however, is to have assembled around himself a gifted squad, including talented designer Don Montague (who has been with Naish for two decades) and a clutch of top-flight riders such as Adam Koch, Chris Gilbert, Mark Shinn, Abel Lago and others, who share Naish's taste for far-out exploits – including takeoffs from clifftops in Barbados or from an aircraft carrier deck in Corpus Christi, Texas.

Prodigiously gifted personalities like Robby Naish inevitably have their detractors and there are some who suggest that Naish is 'old school' and his equipment no longer leading-edge. Be that as it may, the name Robby Naish will be forever writ large in the chronicles of kitesurfing.

Above: *Free-Ride: A sure-fire guarantee of on-the-edge kitesurfing at its most serene and satisfying.*

Left-hard page: *Freedom of movement is the watchword ...*

joyeux

Happy-Go-Lucky

Tahitian Teiva Joyeux was born in 1976, coincidentally the year in which Robby Naish won his first world championship. By the time he was seven, Joyeux was already into surfing and windsurfing, building on the late 1980s media hype that surrounded the exploits of New Caledonia's Robert Teritehau. Teiva took up kitesurfing in 2000, exhibiting a fierce commitment to developing a personal style while at the same time living up to his sponsors' expectations. He took part in a limited number of competitive events but made his name simply on the strength of his appearances in various locations. His style is decidedly wakeboard-oriented and is underpinned by an exceptional commitment to extravagant manoeuvres, not least in his raileys and other radical moves.

When Teiva Joyeux glides surf-style, he goes back to basics, spending entire sessions on surfboards with or without footstraps. That said, Joyeux is a household name in new-school kitesurfing, to which he imparts a totally fresh dimension in terms of innovative figures executed in big waves. In his spare time, he turns to other interests: drawing, music and fishing.

Left-hand page, opposite and double-page spread overleaf: *Teiva Joyeux executes a tail-grab in her unique blend of Freestyle and Wake.*

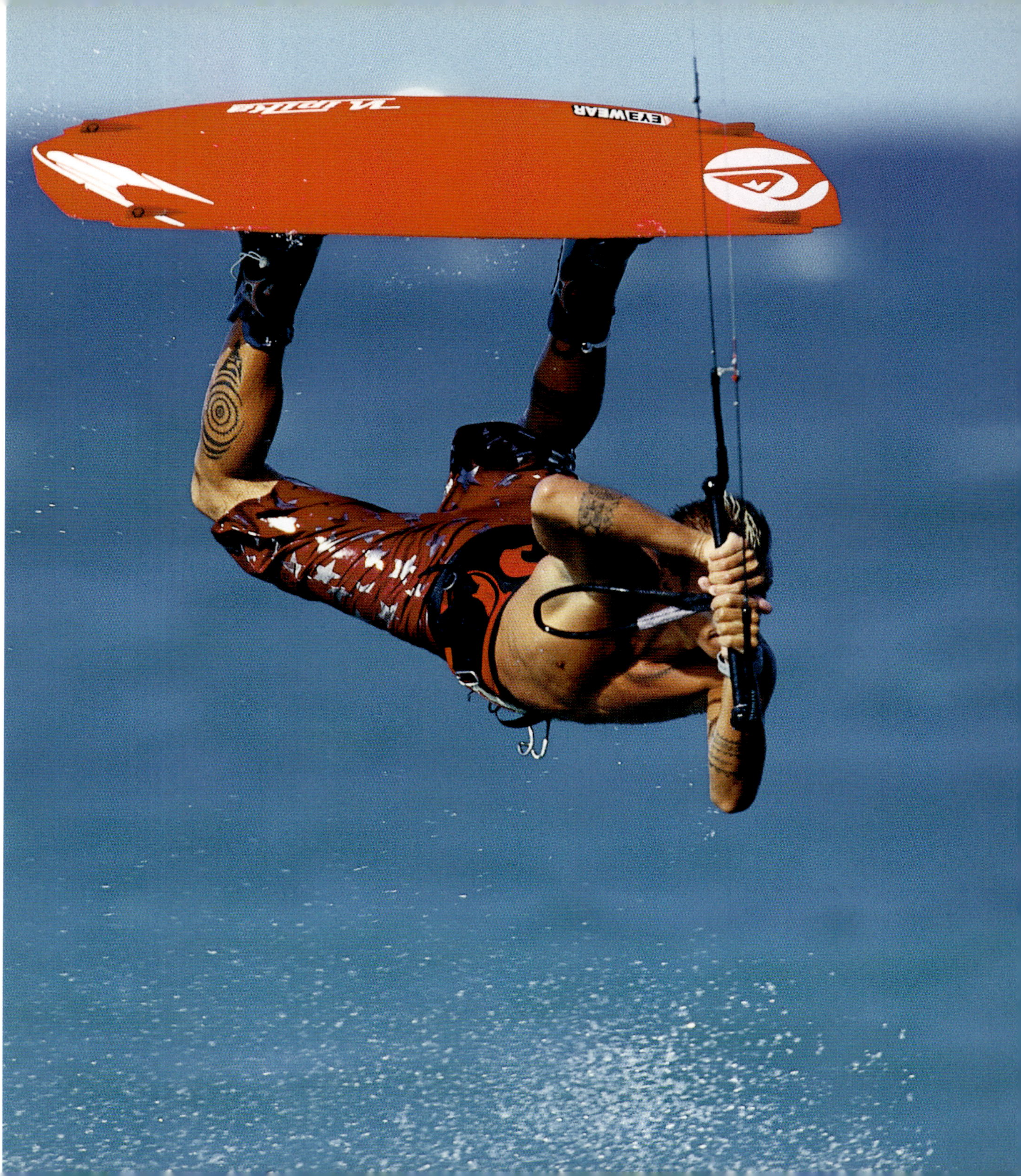

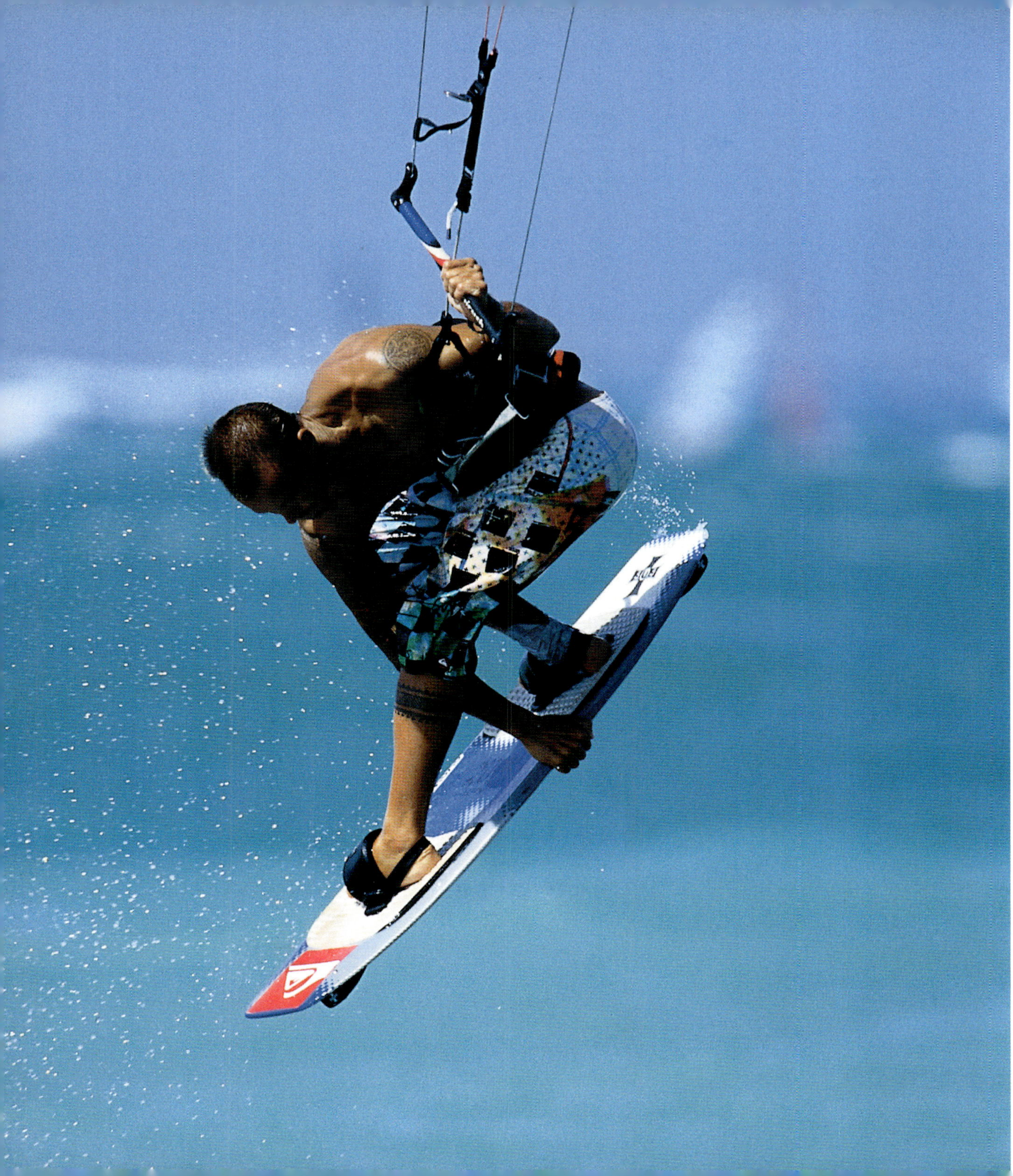

Deleau
charles

Going For It

France's Charles Deleau was born in 1978 and started funboarding at the age of twelve. A twice funboard world junior champion, he switched initially to windsurfing but developed a passion for kitesurfing as soon as he first tried it in 2000. Deleau is now a dedicated kite-surfer who designs and shapes his own boards. Not without success, it seems: as of 2002, Deleau posted his first major results in competition, and attracted sponsorship for his kites and boards. He finished the year as world number two on the Kiteboard Pro World Tour (KPWT) circuit. Charles Deleau is first and foremost a competitor. 2003 saw him rack up four first places on various circuits, including at the Red Bull King of the Air in Hawaii, the Overall World Cup Pro, Red Bull France and at the KPWT in France, where he finished equal first. He built on this record in 2004, when he came first at the Red Bull Pro in Dubai and at the International Air Challenge, which was part of the world championships held in Leucate, France. Deleau's progress has been measured and methodical and his innate professionalism has proved a key component in his rise to prominence after only a comparatively short time as a kitesurfing pro.

Left-hand page: *Charles in board-off mode …*

Opposite: *… and equally at home with a high tail-grab.*

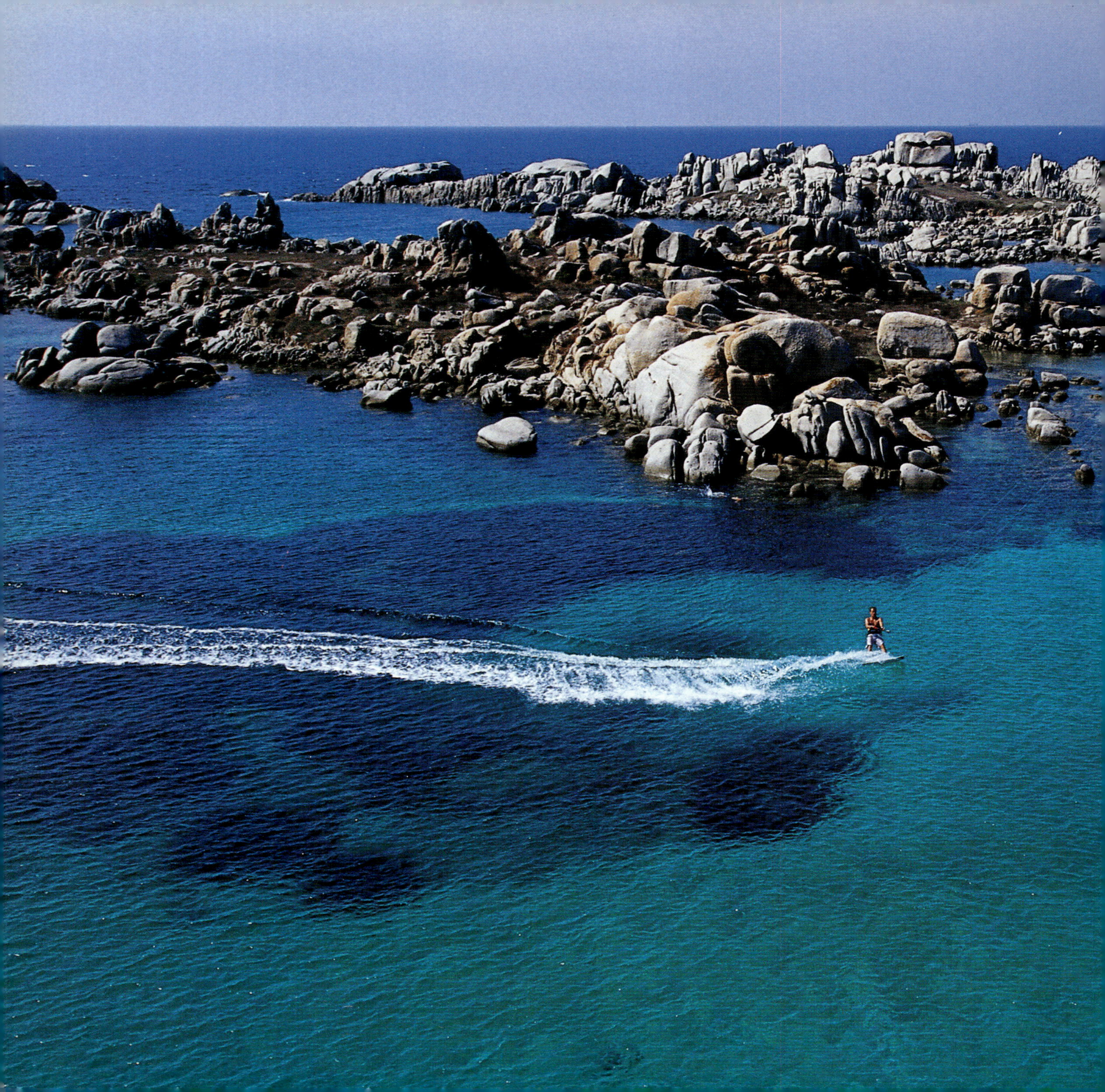

Deleau is a classic example of crossover, and it is no coincidence that he is also a devotee of other extreme sports such as snowboarding and motocross. He is motivated by the whiff of danger that attaches to the most exacting disciplines like freestyle and speed. The first of these is very physical, with moves that are becoming progressively complex and where the similarity to certain aspects of wakeboarding is increasingly evident. Building controlled speed, on the other hand, is now the principal action point on Deleau's kitesurfing agenda.

Time-out for a brief moment of respite away from the pressures of competition.

Vari
martin

Man
of **Mystery**

Twice (2001 and 2003) Professional Kite Riders Association (PKRA) world champion Argentinian Martin Vari lives and surfs in Hawaii. His speciality is moderate wind kitesurfing and he has made his mark as one of today's top exponents in this arena. Vari is something of a loner whose withdrawn personality has tagged him as a 'man of mystery' on the kitesurfing circuit.

Soaring to new heights – and to the world championship title in 2001 and 2003.

salles
raphaël

Pushing the Envelope

Raphaël Salles lives in Montpellier, France with his wife and child. Born in the same year as Robby Naish (1963), his career has in many ways paralleled that of the King from California. Salles was already a top-notch windsurfer by the 1980s, with two decades of boarding under his belt. A French sailboard champion several times over, he took to funboarding in Hawaii and abandoned the classical open board standard in 1983 after winning his final title in that discipline. By 1985, Raphaël Salles was moving up through the ranks, securing a semifinal victory over Robby Naish in a wave trial in Japan and finishing third overall in the World Cup. His experiences in competition and a series of aborted experiments with big boards and big kites convinced Salles that equipment was a key factor, particularly at the highest competitive levels of the sport. Little by little, he upgraded his gear to enhance its ride characteristics. Perennially on the lookout for new thrills, Salles was profoundly influenced by two developments in 1995 and 1996. First off, Laird Hamilton was starting to take an interest in kitesurfing as a big wave alternative to the jet ski; secondly, Manu Bertin was doing his level best (despite the well-intentioned advice of the sport's detractors) to put kitesurfing on the map. Raphaël Salles, persuaded that this was where the future lay, threw caution to the winds and promptly launched his own range of kitesurfing equipment. Salles has been a kitesurfer for eight years now, favouring spots in his own backyard in the south of France as well as more exotic locations such as Tahiti and Mauritius. Technically speaking, his preferences are for surfing interspersed with pronounced kite-loops.

On the business front, Salles is today the CEO of one of the very few companies 100% devoted to kitesurfing. This does not prevent him from taking time out away from his desk to test his own gear *in situ*. His overriding concern is with 'shaping my own boards and developing technologically competitive kite configurations'. He is fully aware that his business will prosper only to the extent that he has a competent team around him to whom he can delegate. He also realises that delegation doesn't come easily to someone who has spent so many years soloing on the water.

He is confident that he now has at his disposal a forward-looking staff that can accommodate different styles and techniques and respond to the demands of the market. His motivation and his sense of commitment are as unremitting as ever. His personal lifestyle, his seafront home and his circle of friends mirror his passion for the sport. His philosophy can be summarised in five words – freedom, thrills, sharing, communicating and passion – and in one unequivocal phrase: keep right on pushing the envelope.

As a seasoned windsurfer, Raphaël has mastered the ins-and-outs of testing his own equipment under the most trying conditions.

d'ortoli

A Seasoned Pro

In the summer 2004, France's Fabienne d'Ortoli became kitesurfing world champion for the second time. These days she seems to make a habit of finishing first. To that extent, she is a natural successor to her compatriot Anne-Laure Pégon, the world's first-ever female kitesurfing champion. D'Ortoli is widely known as 'Competitor Girl' on account of her consistent performances in the French championships and the World Cup. She is, she has had to put her career as a physical education instructor on hold, but her commitment to kitesurfing has paid off with the emergence of sponsors who have taken her career in hand. D'Ortoli's style is multifaceted and geared to the demands of competition. She surfs aggressively yet performs freestyle manoeuvres with uncommon grace and agility, hovering long and high during her big air jumps. The judges have monitored her top-class progress closely. In the quest for optimal training conditions, Fabienne regularly spends time in the Dominican Republic, but she also favours Brittany's Finistère region, where she was first exposed to the sport.

She and a small group of friends initially took to kitesurfing in 1999 on the Quiberon Peninsula. Since then, she has lugged her surfing gear all over the world. Fabienne d'Ortoli gives the lie to the notion that kitesurfing is a male sport. As it happens, more and more women are taking it up and doing the rounds nationally and internationally. In the final analysis, kitesurfing is about technique rather than strength, although peak physical fitness is increasingly important at the peak of what is, after all, an extreme sport.

Of all the women who have taken to kitesurfing, Fabienne stands out, fulfilling her early promise and going on to win numerous competitions. In terms of technique, women are very much on a par with men. Here, Fabienne executes a tweaked invert …

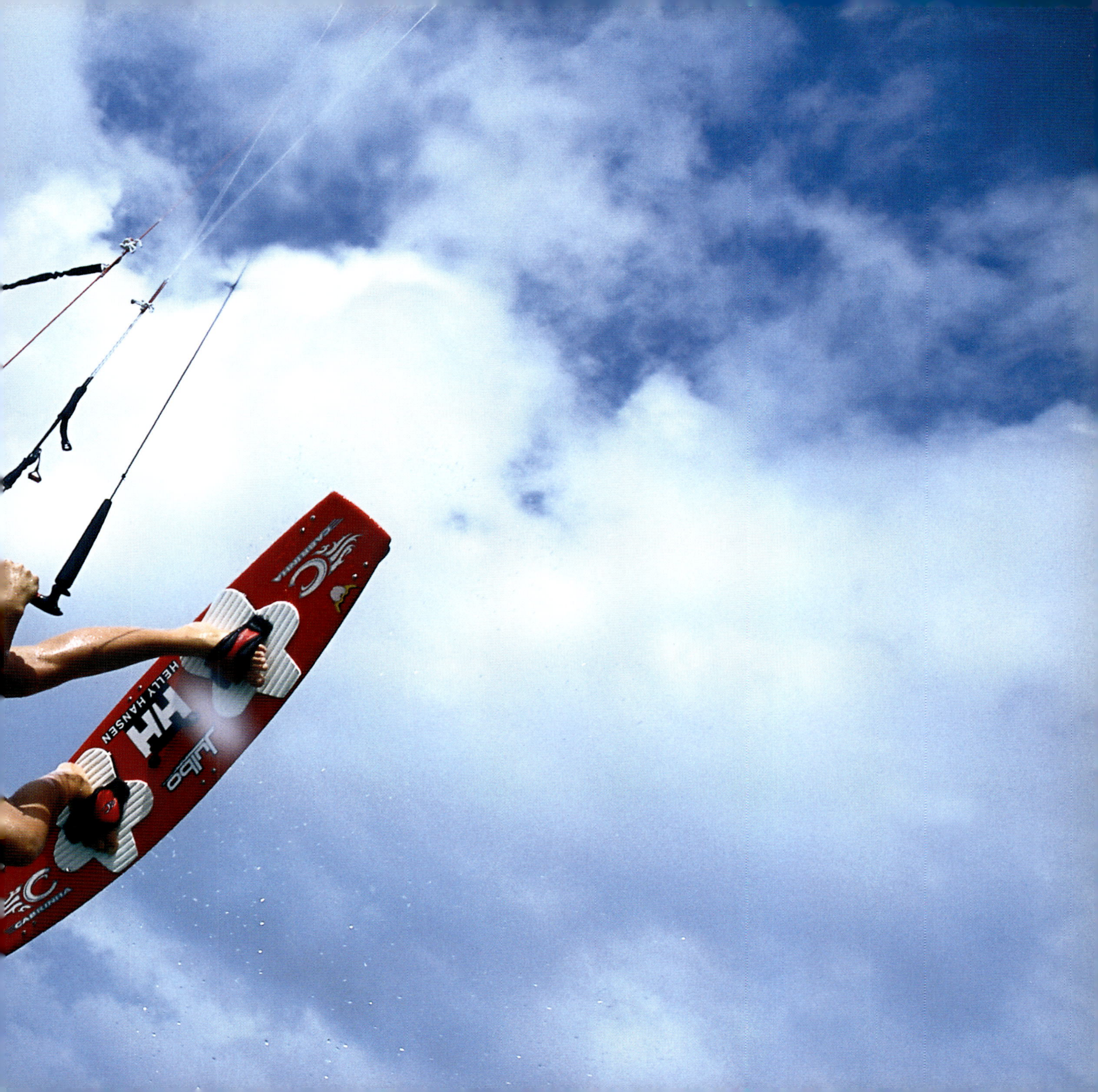
HELLY HANSEN
HH
CABRINHA

consorti
charlotte

A **Lifestyle** Choice

Charlotte Consorti emerged as 'Best Female Newcomer' at the 2001 Boards Awards and as the world speed record-holder at the 2004 World Championships in Leucate, France, where she coolly thrust her way into the ranks of a horde of speed-mad male contestants and, after a few trial runs, posted a 33.24-knot (61 km/hr) ride.

Twenty-six-year-old Charlotte lives a double life, training flat out to improve her competitive performance while at the same time holding down a position at F-One. It is fair to say that teamwork has been one vital component of her success and the technical input of Raphaël Salles another. In essence, she originally set out to compete rather than to win. She had only five years of kitesurfing in the tank and, as a result, was arguably not experienced or physically robust enough to handle the pressures involved. The upshot was that it took her close on a month to recover both mentally and physically from each and every single timed run. But, as has been pointed out elsewhere in these pages, kitesurfing is unique in its insistence on extending the boundaries and setting new performance goals, especially in a sport where official speed times can prove a source of intense pleasure or outright disappointment.

KITESURFING ICONS

Moreover, measuring speed is substantially less subjective than judging other kitesurfing disciplines.

The key to Charlotte Consorti's success is a lifestyle choice made several years ago when she was living in Paris and studying for a degree in sports management. She was a windsurfer back then, with all that implied in terms of weekend travel, freak weather conditions on the coast of northern France, limited time for training and so on. One day, however, she bit the bullet and plucked up sufficient courage to head south and search out windswept beaches in balmier climes. She was still into windsurfing but soon found herself sharing beach spots with the kitesurfer fraternity. Inevitably, Charlotte decided to have a go. She attended coaching sessions in Montpellier and took to the sport like a duck to water. Over time, she has come to appreciate the parameters of the sport, not least the phenomenal physical pressures implicit in speed racing and taking things 'to the limit'. Charlotte is cool-headed, however, and is acutely conscious of what might constitute a danger to herself and to – and from – her fellow kitesurfers.

Charlotte's life revolves around sea and surf. She is frequently to be found at her home spot in Beauduc near Montpellier, but she adores kiting in Brazil and Fiji and at Rodrigues Island in Mauritius. 'It's like a drug,' she confides, adding that, after three days *sans* kitesurfing, she is prepared to travel however many miles it takes in search of 'good wind'. For her, kitesurfing is literally and figuratively a breath of fresh air. She relishes the freedom to go where she pleases, particularly when she chances upon some new spot or other.

Freestyle is a discipline to be shared and enjoyed.

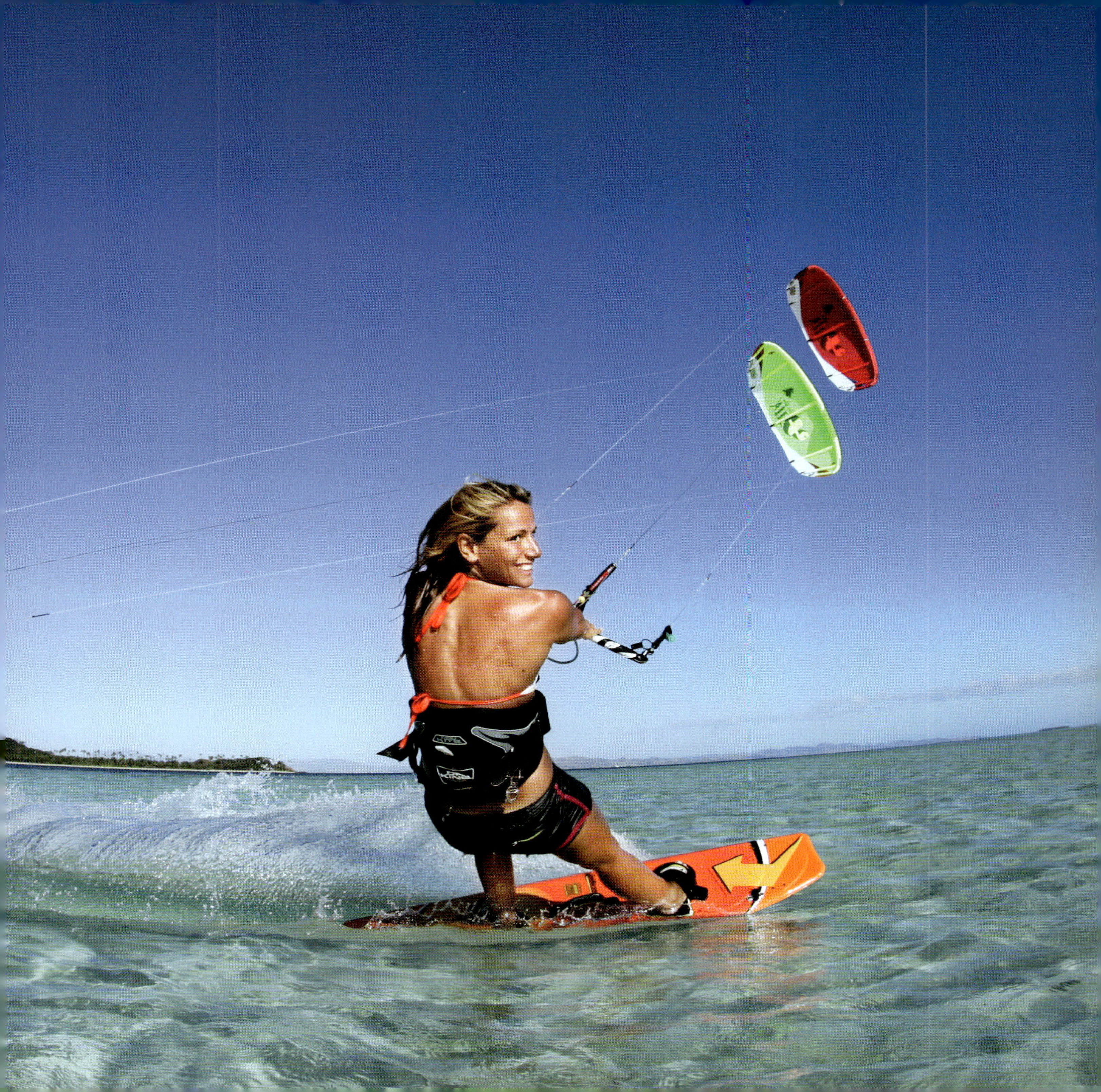

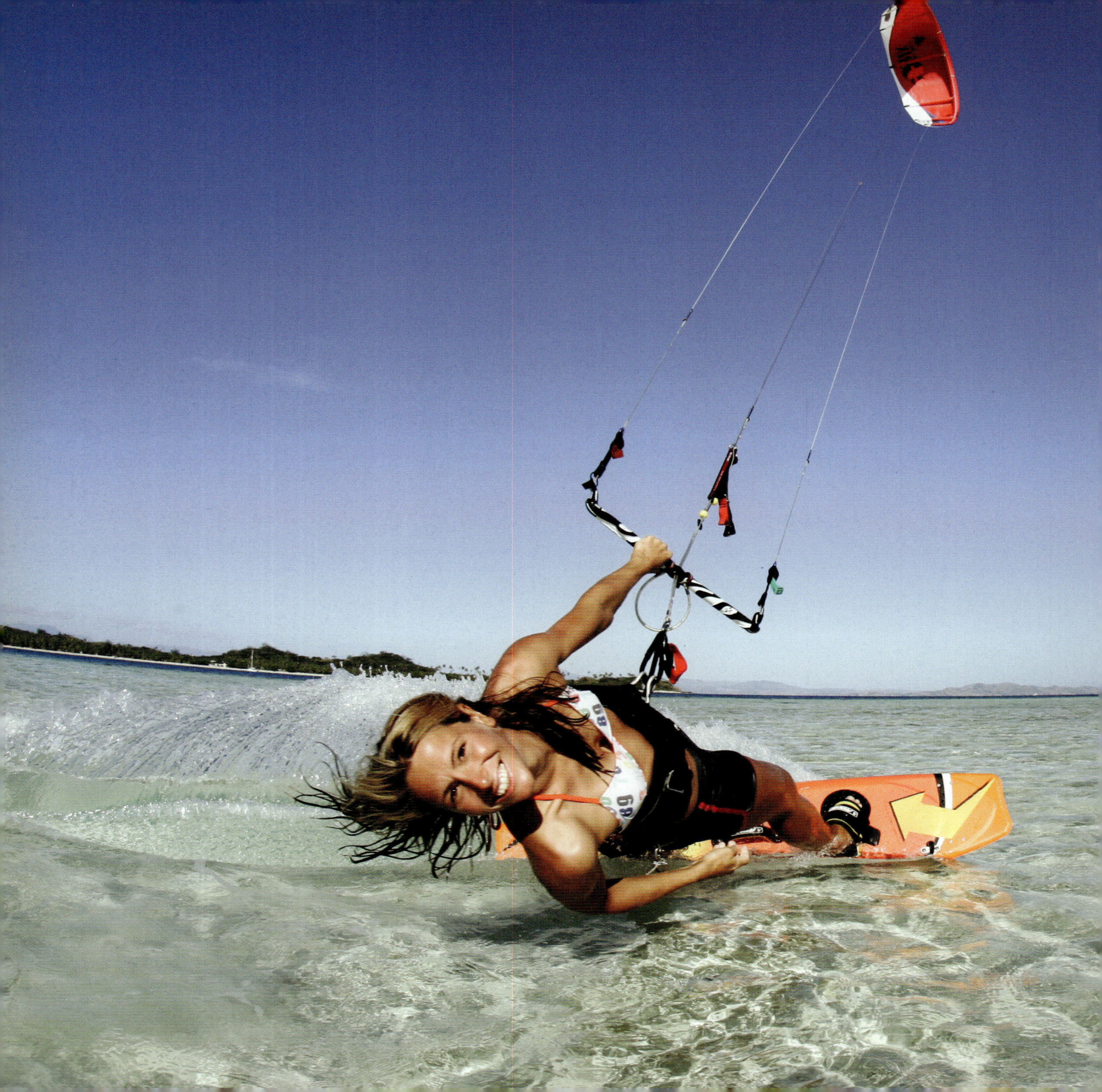

And, even when weather conditions have taken a turn for the worse, she savours the familiar adrenaline rush that is the hallmark of a top athlete.

For Charlotte, job and pastime are as one. She works incessantly, testing equipment and pushing hard to upgrade after-sales services at F-One Kites in a most novel way – from the beach! She is a familiar figure to local kitesurfers, who routinely approach her for help and advice and to swap ideas. This is how she likes it: job satisfaction in spades.

Charlotte Consorti has little free time to devote to other pursuits. She takes particular pleasure in a small but tight circle of friends. As a kitesurfer, she favours moderate wind conditions and rides a 9-metre Dream and a 120 Skate F-One board. She is a safety freak and a staunch advocate of five-line systems. With a lifetime ahead of her as a kitesurfer, Charlotte is committed to using her time wisely to explore new techniques and experience fresh emotions.

Charlotte has made her lifestyle choices and lives the idyll to the full.

La liberté
daphnée

Following Her Star

Daphnée Laliberté pitched up at Cabarete in the Dominican Republic in 2002 with only one thing in mind: kitesurfing. The original idea was to spend a few months away from her native Canada, but the pull of kitesurfing proved so strong that she decided to stay 'just a little while longer'. Her meteoric progress as a kitesurfer is down to her natural feel for surfing generally. She may have started out with no great expectations, but her innate skill has attracted critical attention and equipment and surfwear sponsorship.

Daphnée kitesurfs every day when the wind is right. Even a modest ten knots will see her out on the water with her 12-metre board. 'Light winds are no disadvantage when you're a woman,' she points out. From her base in the Dominican Republic, Daphnée travels to competitions, including some in Europe, but she is always over the moon when she returns to Cabarete for the world championships. Each training session sees Laliberté grinding out and perfecting new moves. 2004, for example, was the year of the 'no-foot' and, as ever, the accent was as much on aesthetics as on athleticism.

Daphnée has opted to live the kitesurfing life and she does so to the hilt, teaching the sport's skills every day for two hours to neophytes drawn to this remarkable spot in the heart of the Caribbean, typically windsurfers from neighbouring spots who are looking for a new buzz.

KITESURFING ICONS

Whether jumping or surfing, navigating the waves gives the feeling of being at one with the elements in perpetual motion.

Daphnée adores teaching the rudiments of a sport she herself positively adores, and she derives undiluted pleasure from the sight of a pupil making the grade.

In the years ahead, Daphnée's career will have two aspects. On the one hand, she will continue to follow her star, building on her skills and developing further her concentration and stress management techniques, and, on the other, she will expand her photographic and video business in the Dominican Republic.

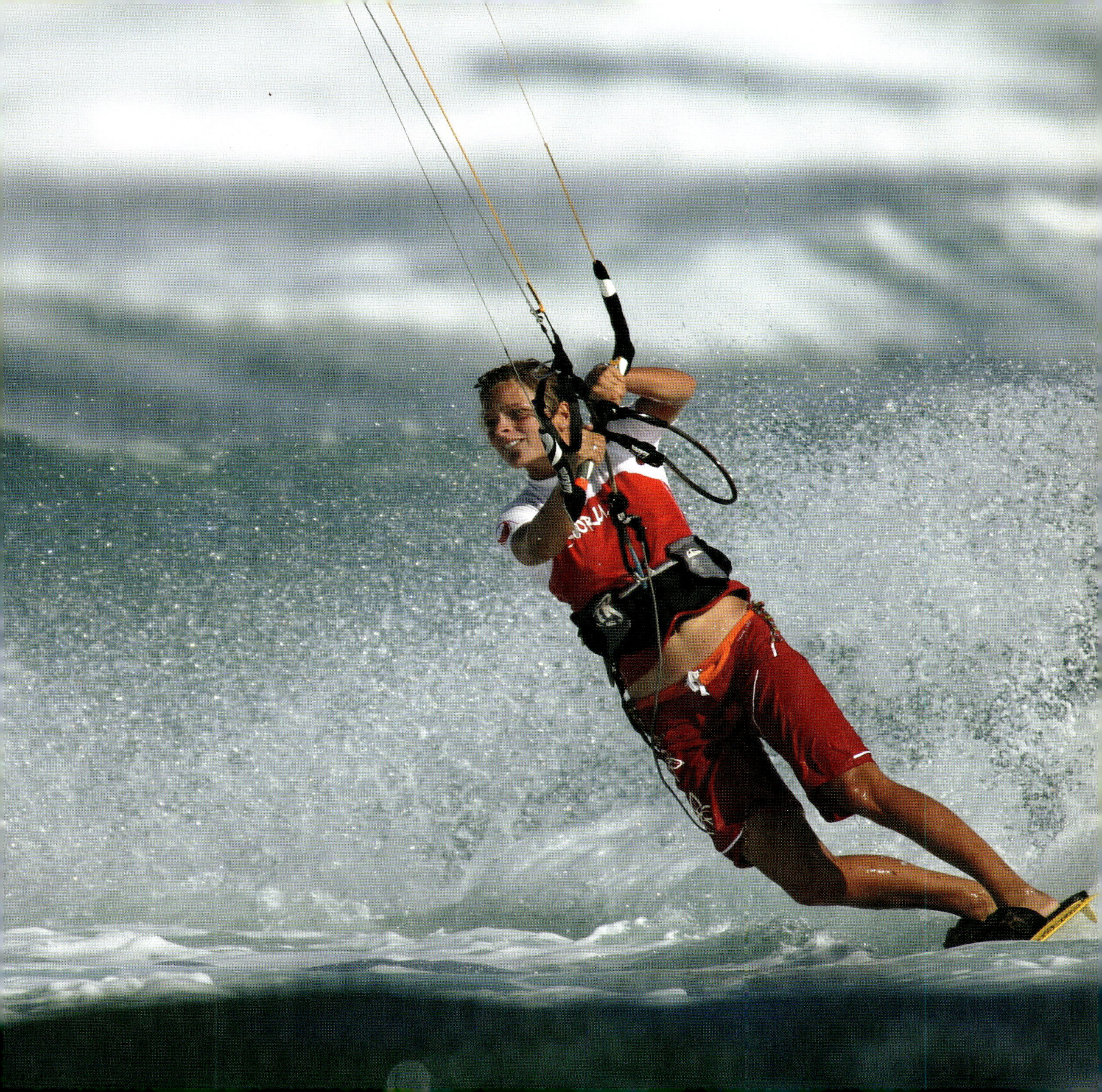

Maui, Hawaii

The islands of the Hawaiian archipelago are by common consent the centre of the surfing universe, an open-air test bed for thrill-seeking surfers. Maui is one of the smaller islands but Aeolus, the God of Winds, has seen fit to bless it with particularly sustained trade winds that blow quite strongly at various times throughout the year. As a result, Maui is windsurf and kitesurf heaven, a Mecca for aficionados the world over. And it is here, in this celebrated Hawaiian spot, that kitesurfing truly came into its own, with its devotees setting out day after day to ride those turquoise-blue waves that the international surfing press routinely extols on account of their quality and predictability.

The number one kitesurfing spot is Hookipa on Maui's North Shore, although it tends to be on the crowded side thanks to previous-generation surfers and windsurfers who flock there. It is rightly famous for its exceptional breakers that vary in size with the seasons and depressions typical of the north Pacific. There is another, more accessible, spot only a few miles off to the east: Kitebeach Park.

Kitesurfers from every corner of the globe congregate here in Maui to enjoy unique wave-run conditions that only the rare few are privileged to experience all year round. Every level of skill is catered for and there is a choice between breaker and smooth-water kitesurfing. This ideal spot is also where the top pros come to train, going through their paces under the admiring gaze of part-timers and legions of photographers. Hookipa is far and away the world's top kitesurfing location and, predictably, the venue for the world's most prestigious kitesurfing events, including the Red Bull King of the Air.

The Legendary Top Spots

THE LEGENDARY TOP SPOTS

Cabarete, Dominican Republic

The Dominican Republic in the Caribbean boasts a kitesurfing hotspot at Cabarete on the island's north coast. 'Discovered' by Canadians as an ideal winter windsurfing destination, Cabarete is renowned for the quality of its waves. Kitesurfing took off here in 2001 and Cabarete's growing fame has since proved a major factor in the island's economic and infrastructural development as a sports and tourist resort.

Conditions in Cabarate are nothing short of ideal, with moderate and regular trade winds, breakers and oodles of space to accommodate all manner of water sports. Cabarete also has its own Kite Beach which is increasingly viewed as being on a par with Maui and is now a firm favourite with Europeans. The World Cup circus visits on an annual basis, contributing to Cabarete's standing and popularity in the microcosm that is kitesurfing. A prime consideration is that the Dominican Republic caters to all levels, from beginners to seasoned pros. Numerous kitesurfing schools have opened their doors and now welcome pupils on a year-round basis. Cabarete's range of facilities has also proved instrumental in boosting awareness of the various other treasures the island has to offer.

Leucate-La Franqui, France

Leucate-La Franqui is a one-off international kitesurfing destination situated by France's Mediterranean coast near the Narbonne Nature Reserve. The surroundings are reminiscent of a large amphitheatre and offer breathtaking views over the La Palme watercourse and out to sea. Leucate has next to nothing in common with other hotspots around the world: there are no waves of any note here, only acre upon acre of fine sand and millpond-smooth water stretching some 16 kilometres towards the coast. Strong winds blow from the mountains to the north and, in spring especially, the *tramontana* blows offshore from the northwest. In summer, the wind direction veers to blow from the southeast.

Visiting Leucate is always a treat, but one's first visit has its own special magic. This is where the Mondial du Vent championship takes place, a major event on the water-sports calendar that brings together all the top international players and includes speed and freestyle kitesurfing competitions. Records are broken year after year, but there's still a feeling of suspense.

Ponta Preta, Cape Verde Islands

Surfing in Ponta Preta is like surfing in a sand desert dotted with volcanic outcrops. The translucent blue water is 'glassy' with magnificent subaquatic contours. Ponta Preta is a famous surfing venue which hosts major international events. Geographically speaking, it may not be at the edge of the world, but it certainly feels like it, situated as it is on the minuscule island of Sal in the heart of the Cape Verde archipelago, smack bang in the middle of the North Atlantic. Prevailing south to southwest winds are the order of the day from October to June.

In Ponta Preta, it is not a question of 'waves' but rather a matter of two distinct wave types – one running right and the other, running left, a surfer's wave that crests in a range from 1.5 to 4 metres and extends typically to about 300 metres in length. The latter wave is often referred to as 'optional', another way of saying it should only be attempted by experts (or die-hard kamikazes). On some days, the area is jam-packed with surfers and windsurfers but, for all that, Sal Island is still a place to head for if you feel like getting away from it all.

Tarifa, Spain

Since the advent of kitesurfing, this spot on the Atlantic coast at the extreme southern tip of Europe's coastline has proved a major draw by virtue of the high wind speeds recorded there. The moderate *poniente* blows mainly in the winter months and results in modest waves, whereas the *levante* is a very strong wind that blows predominantly in summer and justifies Tarifa's reputation as Europe's 'wind capital'.

Tarifa sits fair and square on the Mediterranean, a stone's throw from Morocco, and it is difficult to resist the temptation to traverse the Straits of Gibraltar. Meanwhile, Tarifa itself has quite a lot to offer – notably a bustling and vigorous nightlife which kitesurfers as a rule tend to enjoy. On a more serious note, Tarifa and the surrounding region are sufficiently rich in history to make even an enforced day on the ground a rewarding experience.

THE LEGENDARY TOP SPOTS

North and South Brazil

Brazil has enjoyed the limelight ever since kitesurfing came of age, notably by virtue of the annual competitions staged there. Be it north or south Brazil, there are more top spots on the Brazilian coastline than one can shake a stick at: a dozen or so world-class destinations are grouped on one single 40-kilometre stretch of uninterrupted beach alone. Trade winds and Atlantic swells are the order of the day between Rio de Janeiro and Cabo Frio or between Fortaleza and Jerricoacoara, where white sand and turquoise sea are virtually deserted and unspoilt. To the south, the trades are less pronounced and, as a rule of thumb, the wind is more constant the more one moves north, reaching up to 30 knots at times. Generally speaking, the wind is east side shore, side onshore or side offshore and, as a result, it lends itself to kilometre-long downwind runs. Here, it is possible to spend a whole afternoon kitesurfing without ever having to attempt a single jump. Brazil is a hot topic among kitesurfers and 2005 promises to be the year when the country's full potential comes to the attention of a broader public.

The Cape, South Africa

Picture yourself in the southern hemisphere near the Cape of Good Hope and try to imagine the agonising choice: which is it to be? The Atlantic or the Indian Ocean? South Africa is chock-full of hot kitesurfing spots, each even more impressive than the last. The towering heights of Table Mountain afford an ideal vantage point to identify the region's best locations.

All in all, it is safer to kitesurf the Atlantic coast, given that the sharks there are less aggressive. The wind is chiefly side-by-side offshore from south southeast. On the Indian Ocean side, squalls are possible – but there will be more surfers there than predators. On that coast, the wind is predominantly southwest and occasionally southeast and the level of difficulty is higher, given that waves sometimes crest at up to 2 metres, the result being that the kitesurfer has to know how to go with them or turn back north to outrun them.

Windsurfer pioneers, particularly from Germany and Holland, were the first to gravitate to the Cape, but kitesurfers are rapidly gaining a firm foothold here. The best time of the year to meet up with them is from December to March.

'Jaws': Manu Bertin (December 2000).

The Ultimate

'Jaws' (Maui, Hawaï)

When all is said and done, 'Jaws' is incontestably the one single wave that every surfer aspires to take on head-to-head. This internationally acclaimed giant breaks on the Maui's North Shore when the swell is at its heaviest and travelling in the right direction. Seventeen to twenty seconds elapse between each wave and the jaw-like configuration at its zenith is best appreciated from the North Shore. At times, the wave crests at building height – a magnificent sight, let it be said, but one that spells grave danger for those who are not in the know. In any case, the exact location of the Big One is jealously guarded and difficult to find.

'Jaws' attracts all manner of water-sports enthusiasts, including windsurfers, tow-surfers and kitesurfers, although it should be said that the phenomenon appears only on increasingly rare occasions. Just as well, perhaps, since only the level of expertise needed to take it on shields it against the pretensions of the common herd.

Learning the Craft

Learning to kitesurf is not simply a question of taking a couple of lessons here and there. Far from it: kitesurfing is a serious affair and has to be treated as such. All manner of issues have to be taken into account besides the sheer pleasure of the sport (which, after all, is the prime motivating factor).

Kitesurfing ranks as an extreme sport – in other words, a leisure-time activity that is not without danger, and the growing popularity of the sport presents problems. The danger comes not only from one's own shortcomings and errors of judgement; it also occurs when one's lines and kite come too close to those of another kitesurfer or to obstacles on the ground or in the water. It follows that taking up kitesurfing implies an undertaking to respect universal rules which apply to the sport and which are there to prevent serious injuries or even fatalities.

Like other extreme sports such as canyoning or paragliding, kitesurfing is a 'committed' sport in the sense that, once you commit, you cannot know for certain how, when and where you will touch down. That being the case, the overriding priority is to evaluate your immediate environment and take every precaution to reduce the risk factor to something approaching zero. In other words, before you push off, *check*. Check your surroundings. Check the weather forecast. Check the direction of the current. Check with other kitesurfers who know the spot. Being unsure or on your own are two very good reasons to call a run off.

Not least, monitor your own condition and reactions, checking for anything unusual or anomalous. Human beings have a built-in sense of self-protection. There is nothing worse – nor more stupid – than to ignore the telltale symptoms.

Kitesurfing safely: Checking the weather and understanding and anticipating sudden climatic change are fundamental considerations.

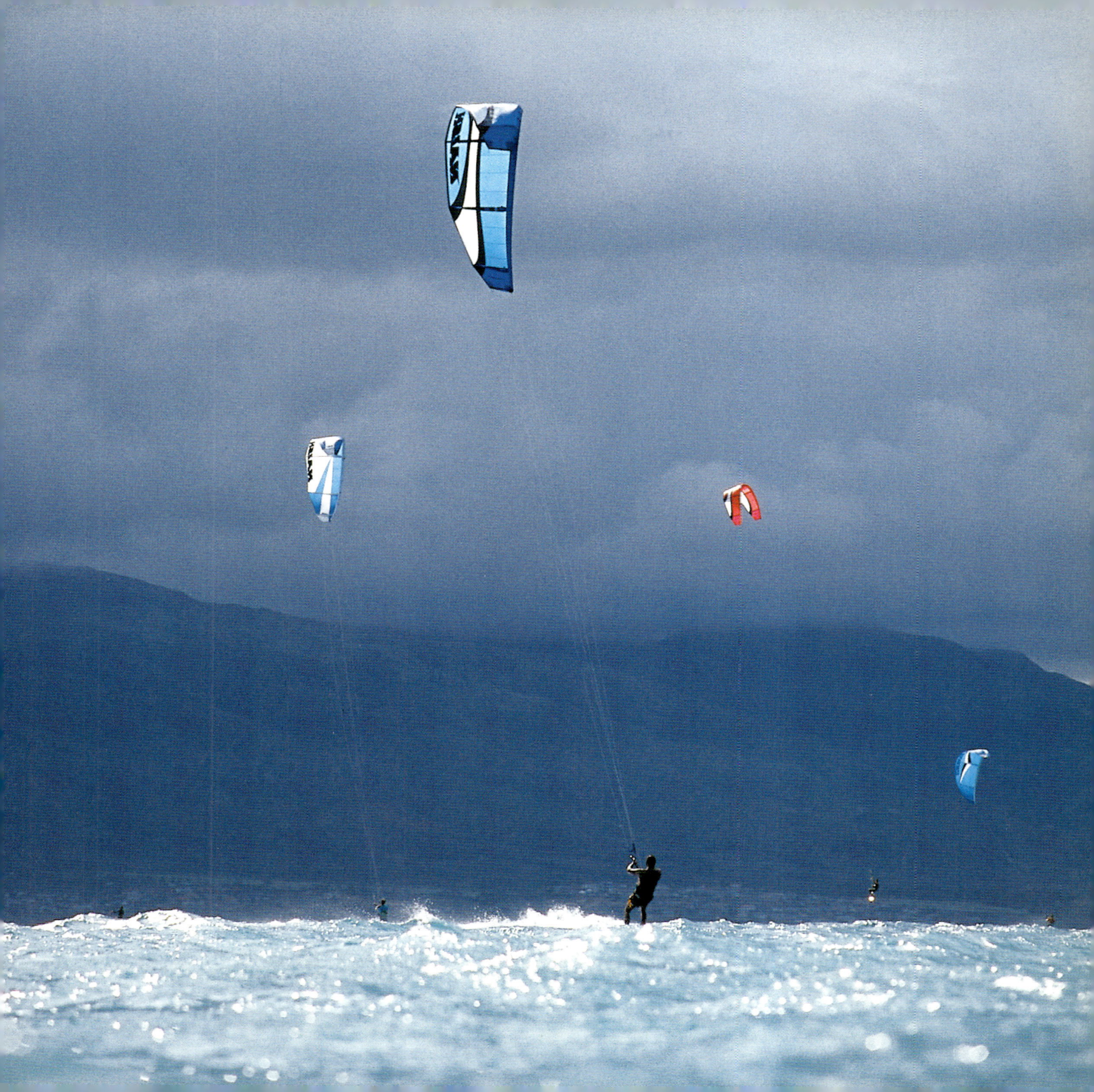

Do It **Right** or **Not at All!**

Readers who feel inspired by this book to take on a new challenge must follow their own instincts. There are schools all over the world where you can be introduced to risk-free kitesurfing and it is strongly advised that you seek out professional instruction before taking up this extreme sport.

Kitesurfing is first and foremost a question of personal commitment, but, in the final analysis, it is kitesurfing that will choose you and not the other way round. The sport requires concentration, physical effort, perseverance, courage and respect for others.

To put it bluntly: if you can't fully commit, then keep your distance!

The extreme demands of competition: Bertrand Fleury performs an enormous kite-loop.

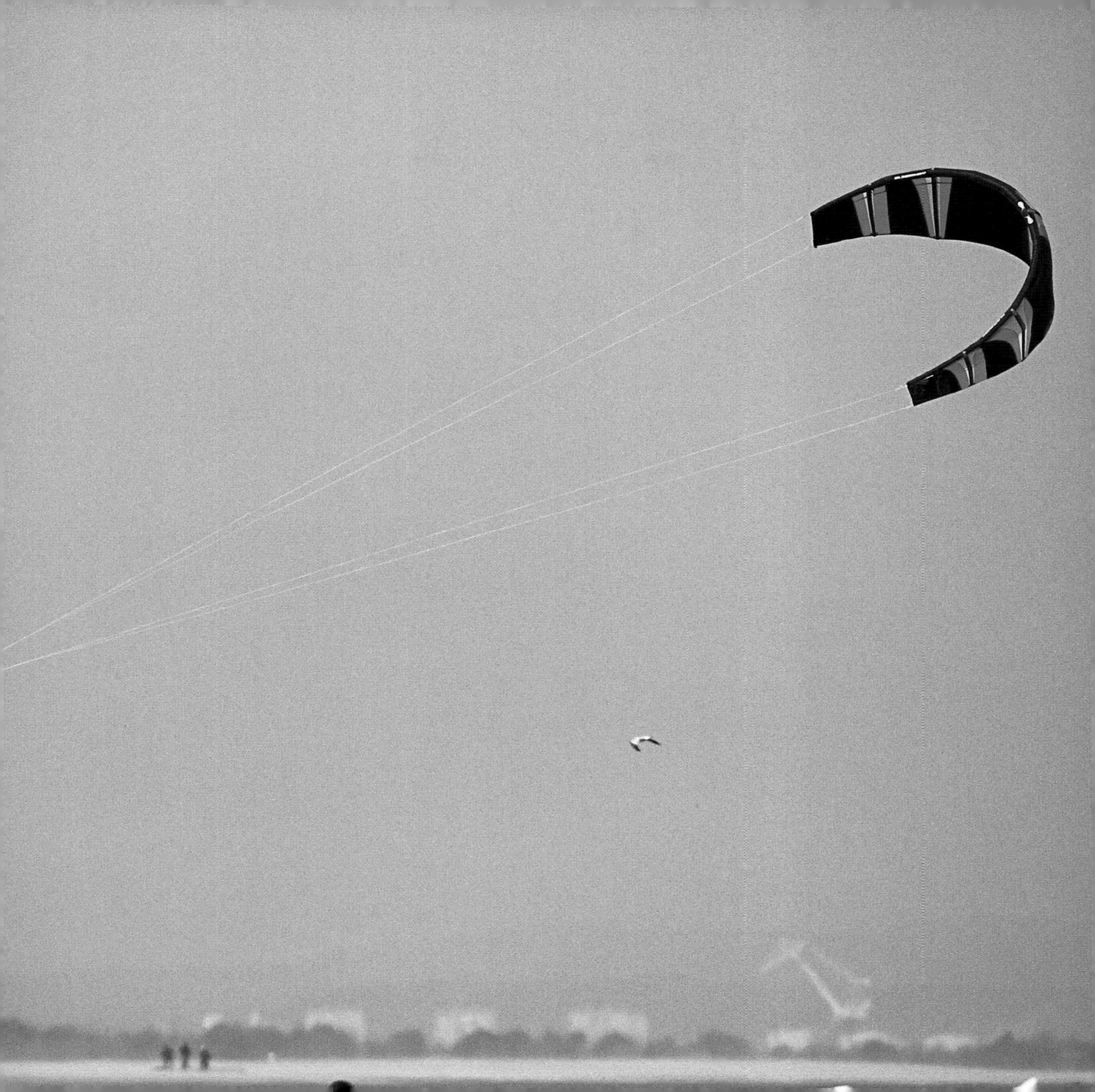

Kite-Speak

Aerial Trick in which board takes off from lip of wave, travels, then lands back on wave face
Airfoil Wing, kite or sail used to generate lift
Angle of Attack Angle at which kite flies relative to the wind
Anometer Device used to gauge wind speed
Apparent Wind Wind experienced by kite moving through air
Aspect Ratio Ratio of kite width to height
Backhand Surfing while facing away from the wave
Bar Used to steer kite
Barrel Inside of a hollow wave; also **Tube**
Batten Carbon or plastic strut enhancing kite rigidity
Beam Reach Sailing in a direction perpendicular to the wind
Bear Change direction across wind axis to generate increased speed prior to heading downwind
Beaufort Wind strength scale calibrated from Force 0 to Force 12 (0 = no wind; 12 = hurricane)
Big Air Very high jump (Big Air Competition)
Bladder Inflatable kite inner tube
Boarding Selecting a trajectory
Bottom Turn A turn at the low end of the wave face
Bowl Perfect 'V'-formation wave
Bridle Lines Lines connecting kite and flying lines
Broad Reach Riding more or less downwind
Camber Curve of board determining aero-dynamic properties
Caper Midair figure
Cell Ribbed compartment in a kite
Choke Release air to take off power and decelerate
Close Haul Sailing as far upwind as possible
Close Reach Sailing more or less towards the wind
Close to the Wind Angling into the wind
Cutback Turning on the wave face to regain white water
Dead Man Jump with full-stretch body and head facing down
Directional Board Board designed to be ridden in one direction
Double Front Board-Off Two-front-loop jump with both feet leaving board
Double Spin Jump with both feet leaving board while it rotates 720° around its own axis and is caught by the fins
Downwind Direction that the wind is going towards
Drag Resistance to movement
Drift Sideways movement due to the action of the wind on the kite
Edge To tilt board on edge to control travel direction
Eye of the Wind Direction wind travels from
Face Unbroken forward-facing portion of a wave

Appendices

Fakie Riding backwards
Fin Small vertical stabiliser affixed to board underside
Fly Lines Principal lines between kite and rider
Forehand Facing towards the wave
Goofy Surfer who extends the right leg forward while riding
Grabber Aerial move in which hand grabs board
Green Room The ultimate in surfing
Handles Alternative to **Bar** to fly kite
Handle Pass Behind-back switch of hands in a jump
Hard Rail Sharp board edge for improved upwind performance
Heelside Side of the board where the heels are
Hooked When rider bar is connected to harness
Indy Grab Jump in which board is grasped with two hands
Jibe Change direction by turning downwind and continuing until a rider is travelling in the opposite or different direction
KGB 360° backroll with handle pass
Kiteloop Kite performs a complete revolution in air
KPWT Kiteboard Pro World Tour
Leading Edge The **Windward** side of the kite
Leash Strap connecting surfer and board
Leech Lines Run inside trailing edge of kite, limiting vibration/noise
Leeward Away from the wind
Lift Upward force which wind exerts on kite
Lift-to-Drag Ratio Measure of kite efficiency
Lines two, four or five synthetic lines able to take 300 kg pressure
Link Line Runs between two **Handles**, enabling harness to take kite load, for one-hand or no-hands flying
Lock In Flying kite straight in direction of travel
Loop Air jump (frontloop or backloop); see also **Kiteloop**
Luff Luffing occurs when airflow to kite stalls
Lull Temporary drop in wind strength
Moves Jargon for figures and acrobatics
Mutant Small-dimensioned directional board with several fins
No-Foot Move in which feet leave and return to board
Nose Front end of board
Offshore Wind blows from shore towards the water
Off-Wind Sailing with a following wind
Onshore Wind blows from the water towards the shore
Off the Lip Re-launching from the crest of a wave
On the Street Super-powerful
Overpowered Kite too powerful for a rider or the wind
PFD Personal Flotation Device (i.e., lifejacket)
Pitrose Midair figure
PKRA Professional Kite Riders' Association
Planing Skimming across the water surface
Pointing Travelling upwind as far as possible
Port Left side seen from a rider looking forward
Port Tack Sailing with the wind from the left
Rail Edge of the board

APPENDICES

Railey Forward jump with: pelvis above head, legs extended, body brought parallel with water
Reaching Sailing across the wind
Regular Riding with left leg extended forward
Relaunching Pilot steers kite off the water and back into the air
Right of Way Tipically reserved for right-hand-forward riders
Rocker Curve along board underside
Run Travel in a straight direction
S-Bend Midair figure (**Railey** with twist)
Scoop Board profile as seen from the front
Sending Suddenly changing direction to generate a power surge
Shape Board configuration by type, lift, keel design, category, etc.
Shaper Board maker (typically by hand)
Sheeting In Increases line tension to put on power and increase Angle
Sheeting Out Decreases line tension to reduce power and Angle of Attack
Side Offshore From the land side
Side Onshore From the water side
Side Shore Parallel to the beach
Snap (Shackle) Quick-release metal fixture
Shorebreak Wave that breaks on the beach
Soft Rail Rounded board edge
Spinout Loss of grip causing board to slip sideways
Spot Well-known or recommended kitesurfing area destination
Spreader Bar Set in front of kitesurfer's harness
Stalling Losing lift (and falling)
Starboard Right side from the perspective of a rider looking forward
Starboard Tack Sailing with the wind coming from the right
Table Move in which rider hangs upside down
Tack Direction of travel; or turning upwind
Tail Grab Jump move in which the hand grasps the board tail
Tantrum Jump move with forward rotation, back turned against the direction of travel
Thruster Fin configuration at back of board
Toeside Riding on the edge where the toes are positioned
Trailing Edge Back edge of the kite running between the wing tips
Tricks Moves involving jumps and changes in direction; augments degree of difficulty
Trim Loop Positioned at centre of control bar; used to adjust kite's **Angle of Attack**
Twin Tip Symmetrical board which rides well in either direction
Unhooked Sailing with harness unattached
Upwind In the direction the wind is coming from
Windmilling Tangling kite lines on some foreign object; prelude to a crash
Windward Towards the wind
Wind Window A kite's optimal 'usable wind'
Wing Kite minus lines; 'kite' in surfing jargon
Wipe Out Terminate a ride involuntarily
Wrist Leash Optional safety leash
Zenith Highest point in the sky directly overhead

Further Reading

Books

Éric Beaudonnat, *S'initier et progresser (Getting Going, Getting Better)*, Amphora Editions, Paris, 2004. Éric Beaudonnat has been a kitesurfer since 1997 and is a co-founder of the International Kitesurfing Organisation (IKO)

Manu Bertin, *De la mer jusqu'au ciel (From Sea to Sky)*, World Traveller Series, Arthaud Editions, Paris, 2003. Authored by Manu Bertin, globetrotter and adventurer *extraordinaire*

Éric Marson, *Kiteboard,* with photo illustrations by Manu Morel, Extreme Sports Series, Arthaud Editions, Paris, 2003

Magazines and Periodicals

Australia: *Freesail* – Canada: *SBC Kiteboard* – France: *Kiteboarder; Kitesurf Magazine; Stance* – Germany: *Kiteboarding; Kitesurf Magazine* – Italy: *Kiteboard* – Netherlands: *Kitesurf* – Spain: *Fuerza 7; Surfavela* – United Kingdom: *Kitesurf; Kiteworld Mag* – United States: *Kiteboarding*

DVD Documentaries

Apprendre le kitesurf (Learning to Kitesurf) by Dalil Abadou Meziani (European Zone)
Vague influence (On the Right Wavelength) by Manu Bertin, Les Archers Editions, Taravana, 2001

Action DVDs and VHS

King of the Bay, Midnight Productions, 2004
Fluid Revolution, Raging Nation Productions, 2003
The Power Zone 2: The Power Trip, Premier Productions, 2003
The Power Zone, Premier Productions, VHS, 2002
Strung Out, Side-Off Video, 2002

Websites

Weather
www.windguru.cz
www.weatheronline.co.uk
www.windfinder.com
www.shom.fr (worldwide waves and times in real-time)
www.cotweb.com
www.sextan.com
www.meteo-marine.com (worldwide sea forecasts)
www.relais-voile.net (sea forecasts for France, Germany and the United Kingdom)
www.noaa.gov
www.oceanweather.com

Newscasts
www.seasailsurf.com
www.agoride.com
www.surfineurope.net
www.webriding.com
www.flysurf.com
www.fpl44.com
www.sickair.co.uk
www.kiteworld.net

Photo Galleries and Videos
www.kitehigh.nl
www.kiteflix.com
www.tronolone.com
www.kiteboarding.be
www.sailriders.com
www.windgirls.com

Forums
www.kitesurf.fr
www.kiteboard.ch
www.kiteforum.com

Selected Organisations
www.pkra.info
www.ikorg.com
www.ibsfr.com/annu.flysurf.fr
www.kitezone.co.uk
www.realkiteboarding.com

Patents
www.inflatablekite.com

Portals
www.sail-online.fr
www.cabaretekiteboarding.com

Acknowledgements

The author wishes to express his gratitude to:
His partner; his family; Kiki and Maman; Charlotte Consorti, Raphaël Salles, Manu Morel, Jérôme Houyvet, Damien Burnel, Pierrot and JC, Christian.

The publishers wish to thank:
Manu Bertin for his invaluable help.

Photographic credits

Sylvain Cazenave 6-7, 10, 33.
Christophe Graillot 111.
Jérôme Houyvet 20-21, 35, 61r., 66-67, 72-73, 74, 75, 76, 77, 78, 79, 80, 81, 82, 83, 84-85.
Jonoknight 18-19.
Manu Morel cover, 4-5, 12, 16-17, 22-23, 24, 25, 26-27, 28, 29, 30, 31, 32, 34, 36, 37, 38-39, 40, 42, 43, 44-45, 46, 48-49, 50, 51, 52, 53, 54-55, 56-57, 58-59, 60, 61l., 64, 65, 68-69, 70, 88, 89, 90-91, 96, 97, 98-99, 100-101, 102, 103, 104, 105, 106-107, 108, 109t., 110, 113, 114-115, 116-117, 118-119.
Kristen Pelou 13, 14-15, 62-63, 86, 87, 92, 93, 94-95, 109b, 112.
Mathieu Turries/Aloaphoto. nu 47.
Arnaud Warech/Norway 71.
Audi 38.
Medicis/RR 41.
RR 8-9.